NICHOLAS WRIGHT

Nicholas Wright trained as an actor. He joined the Royal
Court Theatre as Casting Director and became the first
Director of the Royal Court's Theatre Upstairs, where he
presented an influential programme of new and first-time
writing. From 1975 to 1977 he was joint Artistic Director of
the Royal Court. He joined the Royal National Theatre in
1984 as Literary Manager, and was an Associate Director
of the National until 1998.

His plays include *Treetops* and *One Fine Day* (Riverside
Studios), *The Gorky Brigade* (Royal Court), *The Crimes of
Vautrin* (Joint Stock), *The Custom of the Country* and *The
Desert Air* (both Royal Shakespeare Company), *Mrs. Klein*
(Royal National Theatre) and *Cressida* (Almeida Theatre at
the Albery).

His version of Ibsen's *John Gabriel Borkman* was produced
at the National Theatre in 1996 and his version of Pirandello's
Naked was presented in 1998 at the Almeida Theatre.

His screenplays include adaptations of novels by Patrick
Hamilton, Doris Lessing, Josef Skvorecky and Ford Madox
Ford. In 1998 he received an Emmy nomination for
'Outstanding Writing for a Miniseries or Movie' for his
screenplay of Armistead Maupin's *More Tales of the City*.

His writing about the theatre includes *Ninety-Nine Plays*,
a personal view of playwriting from Aeschylus to the present
day (1992), and *The Art of the Play*, a week-by-week intro-
duction to dramaturgy which appeared in the *Independent
on Sunday* in 1993–1994.

Other titles in this series

NICHOLAS WRIGHT

Cressida

NICK HERN BOOKS

London

www.nickhernbooks.co.uk

A Nick Hern Book

Cressida first published in Great Britain in 2000
as a paperback original by Nick Hern Books Limited,
14 Larden Road, London W3 7ST

Cressida © 2000 by Nicholas Wright
Afterword © 2000 by Nicholas Wright

Nicholas Wright has asserted his rights to be identified
as author of this work

Front cover image design by Scarlet

Typeset by Country Setting, Kingsdown, Kent, CT14 8ES
Printed and bound in Great Britain by
Cox and Wyman Limited, Reading

A CIP catalogue record for this book is available from
the British Library

ISBN 185459 454 0

Cressida was produced by the Almeida Theatre at the Albery. The first performance was on 24 March 2000 with the following cast:

JOHN SHANK	Michael Gambon
WILLIAM BLAGRAVE	Malcolm Sinclair
ALEXANDER GOFFE	Lee Ingleby
WILLIAM TRIGG	Matt Hickey
JHON	Charles Kay
STEPHEN HAMMERTON	Michael Legge
HONEY	Daniel Brocklebank
RICHARD ROBINSON	Anthony Calf

With Mark Rice Oxley and Simon Watts

Directed by Nicholas Hytner
Design by Bob Crowley
Lighting by Paul Pyant
Sound by Fergus O'Hare for Aura

Characters

JOHN SHANK, *an actor*
WILLIAM BLAGRAVE, *a civil servant*
ALEXANDER GOFFE, *a boy actor*
WILLIAM TRIGG, *a boy actor*
JHON, *a dresser*
STEPHEN HAMMERTON, *a boy actor*
JOHN HONYMAN, *an eighteen-year-old boy actor*
RICHARD ROBINSON, *an actor*

Place: London

Time: the 1630s

ACT ONE

Scene One

Music. A neoclassical cloud descends, c.f. Inigo Jones. On it:
JOHN SHANK, a big, burly middle-aged man, now ill. He's
reclining and has a blanket thrown around him.

SHANK. I like the music. Fuck me, what a dull remark.
'Music do I hear?' That's better. That's more like it. As I lie
alone. 'At last I am alone!' No, it was better before. I lie.
Recline. Unheard. Unseen. If anyone woke me, if they
asked me what it was like to die, I'd say: it's like some
hideous long soliloquy. On and on, with never a sign of a
final couplet. While with every word you speak, you feel
more ludicrous because there isn't a bugger on stage to hear
you.

Tries out a speech:

'In Troy, there lies the scene. From isles of Greece, the
princes orgulous . . . ' That's different, that is direct address,
that's *to* them.

Tries another:

'Now is the summer . . . '. Start again. 'My father, lately
deposed as King of France, hath sent this letter. I shall
peruse *in private.*' Who am I talking to? How do I know
they're watching? How in the name of logic do I address a
group of people of whose very existence I am unaware? Do
I ignore them? Do I transfix them with my basilisk eye?

WILLIAM BLAGRAVE, *forties, dapper, descends on*
another cloud. As always, he carries a little briefcase.

BLAGRAVE. Master Shank. I'm sorry to find you ill. You sent
for me.

SHANK. Good day to you, Master . . . Blagrave. At your feet
are seven sheets of paper. Find them.

BLAGRAVE *finds them.*

BLAGRAVE. This is a will. Your will.

SHANK. Well spotted. Read it.

BLAGRAVE *skims a page, then another.*

BLAGRAVE. Did you really pay out thirty pounds for William Trigg?

SHANK. Is that what it says?

BLAGRAVE. You wrote it.

SHANK. Then I did. Thirty big ones pissed away. I liked his style. Bouncy lad with a big loud voice. But he was only any good at saucy wenches. Couldn't touch the tragic stuff. The biggest laugh he ever got was when he went on in 'Titus' with his hands cut off and his tongue pulled out. And his father, brothers, somebody asked who did it. And he couldn't tell them.

He laughs so much he keeps having to stop.

So they put a . . . No, I mustn't laugh, I'll go funny again. They put a . . . Put a *stick* in his mouth. Like a *walking-*stick. And then he *wrote* their . . . God, we laughed.

He quietens down.

I note he hasn't come to see me.

BLAGRAVE. He said he had.

SHANK. Then he's a liar. Nobody comes to see me.

BLAGRAVE. What about Stephen?

SHANK. Stephen would not pat my back if I were choking on my vomit. I gave my lifetime's hoard of craft and graft to that ungrateful toad. I gave what nobody else could find. I gave my heart. And he betrayed it. Stop reading.

BLAGRAVE. It interests me.

SHANK. I can't think why.

BLAGRAVE. It's an illuminating footnote to an unusual life.

SHANK. Skip to the end. I want you to sign. I want you to certify that you are you, that I am I, that I'm not mad and that I've signed it in your presence.

BLAGRAVE. You've signed it already.

SHANK. Bollocks.

BLAGRAVE. Look.

SHANK. No, I believe you. Have you any other reservations?

BLAGRAVE. Stephen was here. I met him a moment ago. He was coming out of the door as I arrived.

SHANK *looks puzzled.*

SHANK. What door? Where are we?

BLAGRAVE. At your house. In Cripplegate, London.

SHANK *looks at his own cloud, then at* BLAGRAVE*'s.*

SHANK. I *am* mad.

BLAGRAVE. You're confused. You've had an apoplexy.

SHANK. More than one, old shiner. Three in a week. And one this morning. Sign.

BLAGRAVE *opens his briefcase, produces a pen, unscrews a bottle of ink. Signs the will. Meanwhile:*

BLAGRAVE. This will is you. It's what you are, it's what you're worth, and in a day or a week or a month at most it will be all that's left of you. What puzzles me is why you sent for me, of all the men in the world, to put my name to it?

SHANK. I have the pleasure of knowing I've ruined your day.

BLAGRAVE. That's not true.

SHANK. Then try another.

BLAGRAVE. What I hoped, was that you'd realised, after all those years of conflict, that I admire you. And that I treasure what you stand for.

SHANK. Are you here to justify your actions or to sign my will?

BLAGRAVE. The latter.

SHANK. Do it.

BLAGRAVE. I have.

SHANK (*disbelieving*). Show me.

BLAGRAVE *hands him the will.* SHANK *looks at it.*

I forget things because I am in a rage.

BLAGRAVE. With me?

SHANK. No, not with you.

He closes his eyes.

BLAGRAVE. With Stephen?

SHANK *opens his eyes.*

SHANK. Trigg was first.

BLAGRAVE. You said you liked him.

SHANK. Listen, will you? Trigg was the first to come *off-stage*. That day. Goffe came next. He was the worst. Honey was best. Till then. But Honey was always ripping his gown to shreds and throwing his wig in the privy. He came last.

They start to ascend on their clouds.

Which meant that Trigg was stuck with Goffe, whose habit, since he could not comprehend the human dramas happening all around him, was to talk in terms which were incomprehensible to anyone else.

They disappear.

End of scene.

Scene Two

The boys' dressing-room at the Globe.

The afternoon's show has just come down. WILLIAM TRIGG, *a stocky, cheerful boy in waiting-woman's costume, is unpinning and taking off his wig.* ALEX GOFFE, *a plain, studious boy, dressed as a Spanish princess, is being undressed by* JHON, *a very old dresser of seventy or so. Both boys are fifteen. Their make-up is crude.*

Neither boy gives JHON *any help, and both have a way of dropping things on the floor and leaving him to pick them up.*

Meanwhile:

ALEX. Where do you keep the lines you've learned? Are they in the picture-gallery of your mind? Or in the library?

TRIGG (*irritable*). Don't know.

ALEX. Are they effulgent images, full of colour and life? Or are they merely squiggly trails of ink?

TRIGG. I can't imagine. Why don't you talk so people can understand you?

ALEX. I'll put it simply. When you're acting, do you think about whatever it is the words describe? Or do you just remember the sheet of paper that you learned them from?

TRIGG. I do both. Like any normal person. And if you're talking about that saucepan speech, I know it forwards, backwards and upside-down.

ALEX. Then why did you dry up half-way through?

TRIGG. I didn't! I was waiting for the laugh.

ALEX. There wasn't one.

TRIGG. There would have been! There was a rustle of breath all over the house, I heard it, everyone heard it, and they'd opened their mouths for a great big *burst* of laughter. And you cut in, you bastard! It went flat on the floor! I'll never forgive you, never!

He throws his wig down.

ALEX. Laugh, laugh, laugh, that's all you think of. You're just a vulgar little show-off. You'd show your bum to make them laugh.

TRIGG. Shut up. Shut up.

ALEX. I dread tomorrow. If you start snoring in the sleeping scene I'll put my dress over your face and fart.

TRIGG. If you do that, I'll kick your balls in.

He pushes ALEX. ALEX pushes him back. SHANK comes in. Same age as before but well. As always, he carries a shapeless old leather bag.

SHANK. Stop this at once! Where's Honey got to? (*To ALEX.*) Goffe?

ALEX. I've not observed him.

SHANK. Trigg?

TRIGG. Don't know.

SHANK. Somebody must have seen him.

JHON. Master Honyman's at the Actors' door.

SHANK. What's he doing there?

JHON. Well by the looks of things I'd say that he's in deep discussion with a member of the public.

SHANK. Splendid. I'll be in prison by Christmas. Before you go, Jhon, on my table there's a case of asinine and aural failure wot needs fixing.

JHON. I beg your pardon, Master Shank?

SHANK. My head. My head for tomorrow. Donkey's head. The company one's no good, I've had to bring my own in. There's a string inside which leads to a kind of seesaw thingummybob which makes the ears go flap. On 'Good hay, sweet hay, hath no fellow.' Remember?

JHON. 'Midsummer Night's Dream?'

SHANK. Well done. Right play. Just look at it for me, will you?

JHON. Is that costume, strictly speaking Master Shank? Or isn't it rather properties?

SHANK. I think that in this case, Jhon, it would count as costume since the . . .

There is a knock at the door.

Yes!

BLAGRAVE *opens the door. He carries a sheaf of handwritten pages.*

Master Blagrave. Come in, come in. Boys, stand straight. Get your hair out of your eyes.

They do. JHON *moves respectfully away.* BLAGRAVE *comes in.*

It is my pleasure to present William Trigg and Alexander Goffe.

BLAGRAVE (*to* TRIGG). The fair Bellamira. (*To* ALEX.) And the Princess of Castile. (*To* SHANK.) No sign of the Queen of Spain? I thought her coronation-speech especially fine today.

SHANK *looks vaguely around for signs of the Queen of Spain.*

Then I must nurse my disappointment. (*To* TRIGG *and* ALEX.) Here is a penny for each of you.

He gives them each a penny.

TRIGG. Thank you, sir.

ALEX. Thank you very much, sir.

TRIGG. May I ask you a question?

SHANK. Keep it short.

TRIGG. Do you remember my line, 'Madam, I trust that fair gallant as far as I could throw this saucepan'?

BLAGRAVE. I do. Though it is not your line uniquely. Many young lads before you have had the privilege of speaking it.

TRIGG. Really, Master Blagrave?

BLAGRAVE. Yes, indeed. I have seen them all.

TRIGG. Well, if the audience wants to laugh there, should we wait for them?

BLAGRAVE. A neat conundrum. Theatrical wisdom, I believe, dictates that one large exhalation takes precedence over many small ones. So my advice would be to continue. What would you say, Master Shank?

SHANK. Oh, absolutely.

BLAGRAVE (*to* SHANK). I'm glad you agree. Now where is Master Robinson? I have a play for him. The author is a man of title and the theme in excellent taste.

SHANK *points.*

SHANK. Two doors down and first on the left.

BLAGRAVE. How does anyone find their way round here? Good day.

ALL. Good day sir.

He goes.

SHANK. The Lord preserve us from well-meaning amateurs.
(*To* TRIGG.) Keep the pause. (*To* ALEX.) Wait for the
laugh.

ALEX. He didn't get one.

SHANK. Because you moved! I saw you.

He hits ALEX *round the head.* JHON *resumes undressing
the boys. Meanwhile:*

Now listen carefully. Master Blagrave, who has given you
those pennies –

He holds out his hand and they give him the money.

– which will be returned to you at the end of your
apprenticeships –

He pockets the money.

– is the Deputy to Sir Henry Herbert, Master of the King's
Revels. Sir Henry reports to the Lord Chamberlain and
there's nobody greater than *him* than the King himself.
And all of these gentlemen rely on Master Blagrave. So
you must neither annoy him nor be too familiar. One more
thing . . .

Another knock at the door. SHANK *calls:*

Yes!

The door opens. STEPHEN *is there. He's fourteen, slightly-
built, unconsciously girlish. His clothes are ragged but
clean. He carries a slip of paper.*

STEPHEN. Master Shank?

SHANK. Who are you? What do you want?

STEPHEN. I come from Master Gunnell's theatre, sir.

SHANK. Come in.

STEPHEN *takes a step in.*

No, come in properly. Where are the rest of you?

STEPHEN. There's only me, sir.

TRIGG. 'Only *I*.'

ALEX. 'The verb 'to be' takes the nominative form.'

SHANK. Ssh! (*To* STEPHEN.) What do you mean, boy?

STEPHEN. I bring a message, sir, from Master Gunnell.

SHANK. Yes?

STEPHEN. He sends his compliments and says he cannot provide you with the five young boys he promised you for tomorrow. Only . . . I. Or me. Whichever it is.

TRIGG. This boy's peculiar.

ALEX. Are we going to have to act with him?

SHANK. Silence. (*To* STEPHEN.) Out.

STEPHEN. But I'm in the play!

SHANK. No you are not.

STEPHEN. But Master Gunnell told me . . .

SHANK. I don't care what he told you!

STEPHEN. But I've learned the part!

SHANK. Which part?

STEPHEN. First Fairy.

SHANK. Out.

STEPHEN. Don't you want to hear me?

SHANK. No.

STEPHEN. Why not?

SHANK. You're wrongly cast.

STEPHEN. You don't know that! How can you possibly tell that, Master Shank? You haven't even seen me try!

HONEY *appears in the doorway. He's a tall, handsome boy of eighteen, magnificently costumed as the Queen of Spain. He sees* STEPHEN.

HONEY. Who's that?

SHANK. Honey, come in. I have a serious crisis.

ALEX. All crises are serious.

SHANK. Shut up.

JHON *helps* HONEY *undress.* HONEY's *hair, beneath his wig, is dyed blond. Meanwhile:*

HONEY. Is it serious like that time you woke us all up in the middle of the night because you couldn't remember the name of the Jew of Malta's daughter?

ALEX *and* TRIGG *find this immensely funny.*

Or only as serious as that boil in your ear that turned out to be a piece of bacon?

ALEX *and* TRIGG *laugh even more.*

SHANK. *Will* you stop? (*To* HONEY.) Honey, old dear, this boy, this child, is all that Master Gunnell has sent me for tomorrow's play.

HONEY. That isn't a crisis. London's full of boys.

ALEX. I could learn those tiny parts in half a minute.

SHANK. First Fairy isn't tiny.

STEPHEN. I've learned First Fairy.

HONEY. Why don't you give him a chance?

SHANK *is unwilling. But:*

SHANK. Oh very well. (*To* STEPHEN.) Begin.

STEPHEN *looks around the room, then gives his slip of paper to* TRIGG: *it's got his lines on it.*

STEPHEN. Would you hold this, please?

He closes his eyes and thinks.

TRIGG. Getting warmer.

ALEX. Any second.

TRIGG. Now.

STEPHEN *opens his eyes.*

STEPHEN. I'm standing under the tree outside St. Paul's. I'm looking at the eight new pillars which they're building there.

The others stare as he remembers his mental picture.

Between the pillars are a hill, a hole, a bush, a prickly branch, some grass, a man with a white face and a bucket of water. Oh, and . . .

TRIGG *and* ALEX *are laughing helplessly.*

SHANK. What are you talking about?

STEPHEN. It's my mnemonic, sir. It's what I use to remember the words.

SHANK. Did Master Gunnell teach you that?

STEPHEN. Yes, sir.

SHANK. Forget it. Nobody learns like that any more. A terrible system. Harder to learn than the speech itself. Just do it.

STEPHEN. Now?

SHANK. Yes!

STEPHEN. With everyone watching?

SHANK. That's what actors *do*, you little squit. (*To* TRIGG *and* ALEX.) Stop putting him off. (*To* STEPHEN.) Go on.

STEPHEN *starts. He's not exactly terrible but he's very inexperienced and his interpretation is excessively fey.*

STEPHEN. 'Over hill, over dale
Thorough bush, thorough briar,
Over park, over pale,
Thorough flood, thorough fire,
I do wander everywhere,
Swifter than the moone's sphere,
And I serve the Fairy Queen . . .

SHANK. Stop! No good. Out.

STEPHEN *starts to go.*

And you may say to Master Gunnell that I'll be calling on him this evening.

STEPHEN (*shouts*). I can't tell him anything, 'cause he's gone.

He's about to disappear through the door.

SHANK. Wait!

STEPHEN *stops.*

Did you say 'gone'?

STEPHEN *nods.*

Gone where?

STEPHEN. I don't remember.

SHANK. When did he go?

STEPHEN. Last night.

SHANK. Did he take any luggage with him?

STEPHEN. Two large trunks.

SHANK. Come in. Sit. (*To* TRIGG.) Trigg, if you attempt to sit you will be soundly beaten, you are still in costume. (*To* STEPHEN.) Now tell me, young . . . young . . . ?

STEPHEN. Stephen.

SHANK. Stephen . . . ?

STEPHEN. Hammerton, sir.

SHANK. Where are you from?

STEPHEN. Hellefield, Yorkshire, England.

HONEY. He doesn't sound like Yorkshire.

SHANK (*to* STEPHEN). Say oo.

STEPHEN. Oo.

SHANK. Um.

STEPHEN. Um.

SHANK (*to* HONEY). I can't hear it.

STEPHEN. I'm telling the truth! I've always talked like this! I can't help it!

HONEY. Ask him how he came to London.

SHANK. Ask him yourself.

STEPHEN. I came because my mother and father brought me. And they signed me up to a draper . . .

SHANK (*mutters to* HONEY). Fucking life story.

STEPHEN. . . . and the draper sold me to Master Gunnell. He got ten pounds for me. And Master Gunnell took me to his theatre. Where I met the other boys. He said we'd all be actors. We'd be little . . . little . . .

ALL. Eyases.

STEPHEN. That's right. He said we'd act in plays. And that one day, if we were good enough, we'd be your pupils, sir. Like him, and him, and him.

He indicates HONEY, TRIGG *and* ALEX.

SHANK. Go on.

STEPHEN. But then he left. And I'm all alone.

ALEX. He's awful.

SHANK. Ssh! (*To* STEPHEN.) Now you're a keen, bright lad. Answer my questions truthfully and I shall give you tuppence before I turn you out. Is that a bargain?

STEPHEN *nods.*

Where is Master Gunnell now?

STEPHEN *thinks.* SHANK *rustles the two pennies. Gives* STEPHEN *one, then the other.*

STEPHEN. In Essex.

SHANK. Where in Essex?

STEPHEN. I don't know.

SHANK. Has he relatives or friends there that you know of?

STEPHEN. I don't know.

SHANK. Why did he leave at such precipitous speed?

STEPHEN. Don't know that either.

SHANK *stands, blasts him.*

SHANK. Out!

STEPHEN. I haven't anywhere to go!

HONEY. He'll starve!

SHANK. Ha ha ha!

HONEY. You're a pig.

SHANK. Thank you.

HONEY. You're an grasping, miserly old twister.

SHANK. True. (*To* STEPHEN). Now look, whatever-your-name-is. You're young, you're healthy. It's a beautiful Autumn evening. Walk through London, spend your money wisely, and I guarantee that Fortune's door will open. Shake my hand.

He holds his hand out. STEPHEN *hesitates. Glances at the door. Then:*

STEPHEN. If I tell you everything I know, can I play First Fairy?

SHANK. Yes.

STEPHEN *jumps up and down in delight.*

Well?

STEPHEN. Master Gunnell went to Essex because on Friday there'll be a meeting of all the tradesmen he owes money to.

ALEX. His creditors.

SHANK. Ssh! How much does he owe them?

STEPHEN. Eight hundred and forty-seven pounds.

The boys whistle.

And he's got no money at all.

SHANK. What happened to the other boys?

STEPHEN. They ran away.

SHANK. Because?

STEPHEN. There wasn't anything to eat.

SHANK. I knew it.

To ALEX:

Goffe, I want you to run as though the hounds of hell were at your heels to the Chapel School. Tell Master Bird to send me ten small eager lads tomorrow at eight, to try for the roles of Moth, Mustardseed, Cobweb and Peaseblossom in the afternoon's revival of . . . Just say it's a play. Tell him

I'll pay him . . . Damn. Damn Gunnell. Thruppence for each boy chosen.

To TRIGG:

You go too. Stand firm on thruppence. Off!

ALEX *and* TRIGG *go.* JHON *follows.*

HONEY. You've done it again.

SHANK. What's that?

HONEY. You've been investing money.

SHANK. Me? What, after the last time?

He laughs.

Ha ha! You must think I'm cracked. Now while I'm . . .

HONEY. I want you to look me in the eye and swear you didn't invest in Gunnell's ridiculous, stupid, so-called theatre.

SHANK. I swear.

HONEY. On the soul of your wife.

SHANK. Certainly not. If she were dead I might consider it. But she isn't. She's alive and living in Watford. She'd be very hurt indeed to know she'd been invoked for oathing purposes by a raddled old tart like you.

HONEY. Be serious.

SHANK. I can't be serious when you're covered in makeup. Look here, Honey old girl, you either trust me or you don't. I didn't invest a farthing.

Pause.

I did.

HONEY. How much?

SHANK. Five hundred pounds. Don't shout. I can't bear it when you shout.

HONEY. Where did you get five hundred pounds?

SHANK. I borrowed it off the board.

HONEY. You're mad!

SHANK. Don't worry. I shall fix it. I shall talk to Dickie. Dickie will help.

He indicates STEPHEN.

Take him through the part.

HONEY. I've got somebody waiting.

SHANK. Work comes first. I cannot suborn the business of the theatre to your after-the-show engagements.

HONEY. He's a Master Brewer. He's invited me out to dinner.

SHANK. I shall go to the Actor's Door and say to Master Brewer that you've been detained.

HONEY. His name is Waverley. He is *a* Master Brewer, comprenez? Portly person. Oh, all right. Tell him I won't be long.

SHANK *indicates* STEPHEN:

SHANK. Do what you can. Try to instil some beef into the lad for God's sake. I'll see you at home.

He goes. HONEY *buries his head in his hands. Looks up.* STEPHEN *holds out his slip of paper.* HONEY *takes it.*

HONEY. This isn't what I do.

STEPHEN. I know.

HONEY. I do acting.

STEPHEN. I've seen you.

HONEY. Let's not discuss it.

He sits back, puts his feet up and closes his eyes. In a monotone:

'How now, spirit, whither wander you?'

STEPHEN. 'Over hill, over dale
Thorough bush, thorough briar,
Over park, over pale . . . ' etc.

End of scene.

Scene Three

The stage of the Globe. A throne and a footstool have been left in place from the show. It's late afternoon.

RICHARD ROBINSON, *a dark, handsome man in his mid-thirties, stands reading* BLAGRAVE's *play-script. From time to time he mutters a line or tries out a gesture. He's still partly in costume as the Emperor of Morocco.*

SHANK *comes on. He goes with purpose to a patch of floor and tests it here and there with his foot, as though looking for something.* ROBINSON *ignores him. After a few moments.*

SHANK. I was certain I felt a nail this afternoon. Ah. No. No. Somebody must have knocked it in.

Pause.

You're working late.

ROBINSON. Mm hm.

He goes on reading. Of the script:

SHANK. Did Blagrave bring you that?

ROBINSON. Mm hm.

SHANK. Oh, we'll be doing it then. Who's it by?

ROBINSON. I can't remember.

SHANK. What's it called?

ROBINSON. Some fatuous title.

He looks back to the top.

'The Coursing of a Hare, or The Madcap'.

SHANK. Oh I don't know. I can imagine quite a run on that. 'What shall we do this afternoon?' 'I know, let's go and see "The Coursing of a Hare, or The Madcap".' What's it about?

ROBINSON. A princess is besieged by suitors, each of whom has to answer three riddles.

SHANK. Oh, original.

ROBINSON. She disguises herself as a shepherdess in order to tell the suitor of her choice the answer. Only to find that he's her long-lost brother who was stolen in his cradle by a crew of Corsican bandits.

SHANK. And is he?

ROBINSON. Is he what?

SHANK. Her brother.

ROBINSON. *I* don't know.

SHANK. My guess is somebody switched the babies. I hate to add to the coils and moils of grey administration, Dickie, but a matter of pounds and pence has reared its head.

ROBINSON. Mm hm?

He turns a page.

SHANK. Richard Gunnell promised to send me five young lads for tomorrow's fairies. But there's only one arrived . . .

ROBINSON. What's he like?

SHANK. Promising. Highly promising. And in the course of . . .

ROBINSON. What happened to the others?

SHANK. That's what I'm trying to tell you. The show is covered, since the Chapel School has boys and enough to spare. But there's another problem . . .

ROBINSON. Let me guess. Gunnell's boys are a penny-ha'penny each. And Chapel boys are . . . ? What are the Chapel boys?

SHANK. Thruppence. Thruppence a show. I don't know why you think I'm badgering you for penny ha'pennies.

ROBINSON *bangs down his script.*

ROBINSON. Because you always do. I've just had Jhon out here about your ass's head.

SHANK. That is different. 'Props or costumes'! That's the creeping canker of the rulebook, Dickie. If I've . . .

ROBINSON. We've *got* an ass's head. It's in the stores. Yours doesn't even work.

SHANK. It fits me better.

ROBINSON. Yes, and every time you bring it in you charge us sixpence. I see the figures. 'Shoes from Master Shank at tuppence'. 'Girdle and gown a shilling'. It's never-ending. You get six shillings a week for Trigg, six for Goffe, eight for Honyman . . .

SHANK. Honey is worth it. Honey is marvellous.

ROBINSON. Honey is now so tall that Eilart Swanston, who is not a small man, wears two-inch lifts to play opposite him.

SHANK. I know that. I supplied them.

ROBINSON. Trigg is a clown. Goffe is a bore.

SHANK. But a very quick study. I always say that Alex Goffe could learn the Middlesex County Records if he set his mind to it.

ROBINSON. If only he didn't make Ophelia sound like the Middlesex County Records. What do you teach those boys?

SHANK. Aren't we're wandering off the point?

ROBINSON. This is the point. I don't believe you teach them anything. You leave it all to Honey. It's disgraceful.

SHANK. May I sit down?

ROBINSON *shrugs. SHANK sits. Silence for a moment. ROBINSON looks at his script. SHANK looks at his thumb-nail.*

You look at your thumb. And then one day it isn't yours any more. It's got ridges down it like a whelk. Then you realise it's your fucking father's.

He looks around. It's getting darker.

For thirty years I've shared my house with boys. I've taught them, clothed them, fed them and I've had so many conversations with the little bastards that I've forgotten how to talk to grown-ups. And what has it led to? What's left? Most of them have left the business. Some play ostlers, messengers and brothers-in-law. Two to my certain knowledge work in steam-baths.

Pause.

Then you. My best. My treasure. You had talent, Dickie. It wasn't your fault it went. That's what it does. It goes. That's why I can't be bothered any more. I teach the bones, that's all. Faster, slower. Louder, quieter. Useful observations, much of the time. I doubt that many, apart from you and me, can spot the difference.

Pause.

I came to tell you something. Gunnell's gone.

ROBINSON. What do you mean, he's gone?

SHANK. He's flit. He's flitted. Flew.

ROBINSON. Do you mean he's bankrupt?

SHANK. I think that's probably how they'd phrase it.

ROBINSON. I'm not surprised.

SHANK. No?

ROBINSON. Not in the slightest. It was a silly idea to start with. Boys playing grown-up men, oh I don't know, there's something funny about it.

SHANK. I thought it had a certain novelty value.

ROBINSON. Thirty years ago it must have. What are you going to do?

SHANK. That's what I'm wondering.

ROBINSON. You borrowed five hundred pounds of company money to invest in Gunnell's theatre.

SHANK. True.

ROBINSON. How will you pay it back?

SHANK. I can't.

ROBINSON. You must have something.

SHANK. I've got ninety sovereigns buried.

ROBINSON. What else?

SHANK. Some wigs. Some gowns.

ROBINSON. And?

SHANK. Are you trying to clean me out?

ROBINSON. I thought you wanted my advice.

SHANK. I tell you what, I'll say my piece, and then you can give me all the advice you want. There's a certain person on the board whom you have influence with. I want you to speak to her. I want her to persuade them not to harry me round the houses for money I haven't got.

ROBINSON. What makes you think my wife can sway the rest of the board?

SHANK. Because she terrifies them. Blimey! What I propose is this. The board can take my ninety pounds. I shall waive my fees and hires till the rest is settled.

ROBINSON. That's absurd.

SHANK. I don't see why. They backed the scheme.

ROBINSON. Rubbish. You proposed it. Gunnell's theatre was to be our nursery-school. You would select the best of his lads and sign them up. Everyone knew you'd take your cut. We need the boys, so the board accepted that. They'd might even accept the utterly ludicrous terms you've offered if you'd done a tenth of what you promised. But you haven't. Did you go to Gunnell's theatre? Did you see his boys?

SHANK. No. I bloody didn't!

ROBINSON. Why?

SHANK. Because I smelt disaster! And it frightened me. I cannot survive it. I'm old. I'm poor. Why do you think I grovelled in the first place? To a board comprised of lawyers, property-thieves and good plain cooks. Who wouldn't know a decent play if it kicked them in the arse. That a man like me should have to crawl to them is vile and wicked. As for your position it makes me cry. You signed a Faustian pact with power. You married Mistress Burbage and it ruined your acting. You dare not open your mouth at home, so now you can't open it properly on stage. Fuck the board. And fuck you too, you widow's bumboy.

He stops, appalled.

ROBINSON. Get out.

SHANK. I will. I will.

He hesitates.

I didn't mean . . . I wasn't suggesting you don't fuck your wife.

ROBINSON. Out.

SHANK *looks at the way off-stage.*

SHANK. Yes. Hm. Tricky exit.

He hesitates.

About my offer. What I suggest is, ninety down, and the rest on tick.

ROBINSON. I've not forgotten.

SHANK. What's your answer?

ROBINSON. Dig up your money. Sell your assets. Pay your debt. It's either that or prison.

SHANK. Done.

End of scene.

Scene Four

Later that night.

SHANK's *house. Large room. A window with a blanket nailed over it. A ladder leads to a hole in the ceiling. Gowns and props are littered around the room. There's a long table with bowls, bread, jug of beer, mugs, etc. At* SHANK's *place is a box and some stage jewellery. Also a filthy, earth-caked bag of money. The spade* SHANK *dug it up with is leaning somewhere.*

STEPHEN *is rummaging through a pile of costumes, looking with care at each garment in turn. He's washed and changed.* ALEX *and* TRIGG *are at the table.*

SHANK *is at the table with a saucepan of stew. To* STEPHEN:

SHANK. How are we doing?

STEPHEN. I'm finished.

SHANK *tastes the stew. To* STEPHEN:

SHANK. Sit.

STEPHEN takes his place at the table. SHANK nods to TRIGG. They all close their eyes and steeple their hands. TRIGG says a learned grace.

TRIGG. 'Almighty God, who made mankind, we thy actors are its humble shadows. Therefore take our acting as our praise of thy creation. We pray to thy Son, who acted the part of a man till death, that we may follow his steps until his voice cries out once more "It is enough." We pray to thy Holy Spirit, to inspire us. We thank thee for our food, and we remind thee in all hopeful honesty that we have none for tomorrow. May we be sober at work, afire on stage and joyful in the acclamation of the crowd, thy creature. And when we are called at last to play at thy heavenly Court, grant that we be word-perfect.'

ALL. Amen.

The boys start eating. Spoons only. If a knife is required, they borrow SHANK's pocket-knife. STEPHEN eats much more than anyone else. SHANK tips the money-bag on to the table and counts out the coins while munching a piece of bread.

ALEX. William?

TRIGG. Alexander?

ALEX. How disgusting is our mutton stew this evening?

TRIGG. Quintessentially.

ALEX. Disgusting of its nature. Notoriously.

TRIGG. Um . . . Famous for being disgusting. Self-evidently.

ALEX. You can tell it's disgusting just by looking at it. Ontologically.

TRIGG. Don't know.

ALEX. Of or pertaining to the quality of disgustingness. Master Hammerton?

STEPHEN. I don't know how to play.

TRIGG. Have a try.

STEPHEN. Archimedes?

The other two boys laugh derisively.

TRIGG (*to* SHANK). I thought you said he was an asset.

SHANK. He will be *quite* an asset. Once I've done his papers.

ALEX. Who in the world would want to buy him?

SHANK. There's always someone.

TRIGG. Nobody's seen him act.

SHANK. That's what I'm counting on.

He puts the money back in its bag and makes a note. To
STEPHEN:

You ready?

STEPHEN *nods.*

Imagine you're back in the draper's shop. A customer offers
to buy the stock. And that is it.

i.e. the costumes STEPHEN *was looking through.*

Now. What's it worth?

STEPHEN. Six pounds for the gown in blue brocade. Eight for
the ox-blood velvet trimmed with lace. Four for the taffeta
suit. Ten pairs of slippers at ninepence each . . .

SHANK. What does it come to?

STEPHEN. Cash or credit?

SHANK. Doesn't matter.

STEPHEN. One hundred and fifty pounds.

SHANK. You're a good lad.

*HONEY comes in. He's adapted his make-up for street
wear. He carries a pair of legal documents.*

Come in, come in. How was Master Waverley?

HONEY. Suspicious.

SHANK. Did he sign the deeds?

HONEY. He did!

SHANK. Let's see them.

HONEY passes him the documents.

Sit down. Have some stew.

HONEY. I've eaten.

STEPHEN. Where did you eat?

HONEY. At the sign of the long, inquisitive nose.

STEPHEN. Where's that?

The boys groan, and:

ALEX. Somebody buy him!

TRIGG. Boy for sale! Boy for sale!

SHANK. Quiet, you two. I'm trying to read.

HONEY. It was awful. There were flowers on the table. It was meant to be a romantic supper. And all we talked about was signing bogus documents. I've never been so embarrassed in all my life. I felt like Shylock.

SHANK. You'll get used to it. (*Of the documents.*) These are perfect. And the news is good. Counting the mandolin, assuming I can get it back from Eilart Swanston . . .

He indicates STEPHEN.

. . . and including *him*, and taking on trust his views on the costume prices, I seem to be worth somewhere between four-fifty and five hundred pounds.

HONEY. That's every penny you've got.

TRIGG. It's every button.

ALEX. We'll have no wigs. We'll have no fans. We'll have no stockings.

TRIGG. We won't even have any gowns.

SHANK. You're actors. What do you want with gowns? Wear the company's.

TRIGG. We'll look hideous.

ALEX. We'll be the laughing-stock of London.

SHANK. Shut up. *I'm* the one who's destitute. And am I whining? Look at this smile. Look at this twinkle in my eye. It is the light of challenge. Bedtime. Get your shirts off.

ALEX (*of* STEPHEN). What about him?

SHANK. He's eating. Come along, who's first?

ALEX and TRIGG *take their shirts off. Meanwhile:*

HONEY. Where's my roll?

STEPHEN. It's here.

He gives HONEY *his roll: it's literally a roll of paper with* HONEY*'s lines and cues for tomorrow written on it.* ALEX *takes up position in front of* SHANK. HONEY *reads.*

STEPHEN. Do you want me to hear your lines?

HONEY. I know them, thank you.

STEPHEN turns to watch SHANK, *who is feeling* ALEX*'s armpits, groin and the sides of his neck for swollen lymph-nodes. After a few moments:*

STEPHEN (*quietly to* TRIGG). What's he doing?

TRIGG. Looking for lumps.

STEPHEN. What would happen if he found one?

TRIGG. The lumpy boy would die.

SHANK. If anyone sees a lump on even one of you boys, we'll all of us have to stay at home. So if I find one, you must keep it a secret. (*To* ALEX.) You were dull today. Remember the light and shade. No two things in the world are quite the same. We'll do some work on Hermia in the morning.

ALEX. You'll forget. Good night.

He collects his shirt, climbs the ladder and disappears into the loft.

SHANK (*to* TRIGG). Come on.

TRIGG stands for inspection. SHANK *feels his lymph-nodes, as before.*

I heard you cough at breakfast.

TRIGG. I was trying a different way of eating.

SHANK. Turn round.

TRIGG *does.*

Tomorrow's play is a good old play. I would like you to respect it. Don't be tasteless.

TRIGG. When am I tasteless?

SHANK. When you play for tasteless laughs.

TRIGG. Which laughs are they?

SHANK. Oh don't ask me.

HONEY. It may be very fussy of me, but I always feel that taste has lost the battle when he sticks his tits out on 'double cherry'.

SHANK. There you are. Honey will tell you. Don't move.

He takes a closer look.

TRIGG. What is it?

SHANK *looks with care.*

SHANK. Fleabite. Off you go.

TRIGG *finds his roll for tomorrow, climbs the ladder and goes out. Meanwhile, to* STEPHEN:

You.

STEPHEN *is about to take off his shirt.*

Lumps come later. (*To* HONEY.) Pass me those. (*To* STEPHEN.) Sit there.

HONEY *gives him the two documents he came in with.* SHANK *and* STEPHEN *sit at the table.* SHANK *selects a document.*

This deed . . .

He checks the signature.

. . . now signed, records that you, Stephen Hammerton, are duly apprenticed to William Waverley, Master Brewer of the Strand.

STEPHEN. I don't want to be a brewer!

SHANK. You won't be. All this is, is proof of ownership. It's like a pedigree. You can't be sold without it. It doesn't have to be true. It isn't true. But you must keep it dark. You know what they do to forgers.

He selects the other document:

This deed records that Master Waverley sold you, Stephen Hammerton, to me, John Shank for thirty pounds.

STEPHEN. Did Honey pay him?

SHANK. Nobody paid him. Honey asked him nicely. And I'm sure that Master Waverley felt sufficiently rewarded. Make your mark.

STEPHEN *starts to write.*

That's not a mark.

He raises his eyebrows as STEPHEN *starts the elaborate calligraphic exercise of a signature. To* HONEY:

SHANK. He writes his name.

HONEY *starts to go.*

What are you doing?

HONEY. I'm going to change.

SHANK. You can't go out now. It's nearly midnight.

HONEY *goes to the ladder, starts climbing up.*

HONEY. Don't wait up.

SHANK. I shan't. Have you got your key?

HONEY *continues climbing.*

I said, have you got your . . . ?

HONEY *disappears into the loft.* SHANK *goes to the foot of the ladder, shouts:*

Don't turn your back on me!

He looks up at the trapdoor.

STEPHEN. I've signed it.

SHANK goes to him. Takes the document and hits
STEPHEN hard across the head. STEPHEN bursts into
tears. After a long while:

STEPHEN. What was that for?

SHANK *doesn't know.*

SHANK. It's traditional. On the signing of the deeds. It's
called a buffet.

STEPHEN. Why did you do it so hard?

SHANK. I slipped.

He glances up at the loft-door.

Have some beer.

STEPHEN. I don't like beer.

SHANK. Have you tried it?

STEPHEN shakes his head. SHANK pours beer, hands it
to STEPHEN.

Here.

STEPHEN *drinks.*

Still hurting?

STEPHEN *nods.*

I'm sorry.

STEPHEN. It wasn't just the buffet. It was knowing you'll sell
me off.

SHANK. I've got no choice. I need the money. I can't spare
Honey or Trigg. And Goffe's unsellable.

STEPHEN. Is it because of the way I do my Fairy speech?

SHANK. Not at all. Your Fairy speech is better now. You'll be
fine. Just remember not to blink so much or jiggle your
hands about.

STEPHEN. I'll try.

SHANK. Good lad.

He pours himself beer.

Where did you pick it up, that girlish manner?

STEPHEN. I don't know.

SHANK (*suspicious*). You've not been hanging about with girls?

STEPHEN. No. I've been like this as long as I can remember. I'm just a little surprised that I'm too girlish even to play the part of a fairy. I thought the Fairy *was* a girl.

SHANK. That's irrelevant. Cast it out of your mind completely. I had a line of dialogue once that says it all. 'Some squeaking Cleopatra *boy* my greatness i' the posture of a whore.' He didn't say 'girl' my greatness. If 'girl' was what he meant he would have written it. He meant a boy, a sound, intelligent boy who speaks up loud and clear and picks his cues up.

STEPHEN. Is that all there is to it?

SHANK. It's what I suggest you aim at. If you want to become an actor.

SHANK. I don't know if I do.

He drinks.

STEPHEN. I like *seeing* plays. Master Gunnell used to walk us in for nothing. And I liked it backstage today. Though I was nervous.

SHANK. Did you never make up plays with your friends at school?

STEPHEN. No.

SHANK. Did you never dress up?

STEPHEN. I dressed up once. Although I wouldn't exactly call it acting. It was last Easter weekend. I'd taken down some curtains in the dining-room. And I'd wrapped them round me. And I was standing on the table when my father walked in. And the very next week, he and my mother brought me down to London. They signed me up with the draper and I thought, 'Oh good, they like me after all.' But when I went back to where we were staying, to say good-bye, they'd gone. They'd paid the bill and left me a pair of shoes. I thought they'd both gone mad. They never wrote. And then one night I met a tinker. He'd been to Hellefield. He'd actually mended their pots and pans. He said that all the time he was tapping away, they were laughing and holding hands. He said they looked as though they'd just got married.

He looks at his beer-mug: it's empty.

Was that just a dash to see if I liked it?

SHANK. Do you?

STEPHEN. It's interesting.

SHANK pours him more beer.

Were you an apprentice once?

SHANK. I was kidnapped. 1599, one week to Christmas. Frosty morning. I took a short cut through St. Paul's, came out at Ludgate and there on the corner I spied a shabby gentleman in a tall hat, standing on one leg like a stork. I quickened my pace, didn't look back, and the next I knew, I felt a pair of arms around me and a sack put over my head. He carried me kicking and squealing through a gate, across a yard, up steps, into a large and echoing room, locked the door, took off the sack and that was my first sight of the Blackfriars Theatre. Where you will play when winter comes. That man was Thomas Evans, a disgrace to the Welsh, Master of the Chapel Boys. There I sat, all day, while every hour or so the door flew open and another boy shot in. Twelve in all. You should have heard us. Screaming, shouting, boys boo-hooing. Most of it came to nothing, because the following day their parents arrived and took them back. Every time a mother and father led their howling child across the snow, I'd say to the boy beside me: 'Mine are next.' I couldn't admit that the only creature on earth who minded whether I lived or died was a shabby gentleman with a tall hat. So there you are. We're fellow-spirits.

He gets up.

By noon there were only two of us left. Myself and a boy called Salamon Pavy. My pal, as the Romanies say. We went to the Globe in the following year. And then he died.

STEPHEN. What did he die of?

SHANK. Boys died fast in those days.

Outside a church clock strikes twelve.

Bedtime. Find a place in the loft. I'm locking up.

He blows out candles, leaving one alight.

STEPHEN. I need a blanket.

SHANK *looks round the chaotic room. He sees a thick cloth hanging over the window. He tugs it and it comes away. Moonlight floods in. He looks out of the window.*

Nice night for a walk.

STEPHEN. Is it really just the money?

SHANK. Eh? Oh yes. Here, catch.

He throws the blanket to STEPHEN.

Good night.

STEPHEN. Good night, sir.

SHANK *collects his money and jewels and goes.* STEPHEN *goes to the window. Wraps the blanket around him. Sits thinking. After a moment, a door is heard closing downstairs.* HONEY *appears at the top of the ladder, dressed for a night out.*

HONEY. Where's Shanky?

STEPHEN. Out.

HONEY. What, properly out?

STEPHEN. Yes, out.

HONEY *climbs down.*

Where are you going?

HONEY. Where you can't follow.

STEPHEN. Why not?

HONEY. Because you're just a kid.

STEPHEN. Is that a Romany word? Like 'pal'?

HONEY. What's 'pal'?

STEPHEN. A friend. I think.

HONEY*'s about to go.*

I'm going out too. Do you want to come with me?

HONEY. Where are you going?

STEPHEN. I'm going to commit a crime. And I need an
accomplice.

Pause

Does it attract you?

End of scene.

Scene Five

*A sauna. Small wooden room. A brazier, a pan of water, a
ladle. Voices and laughter heard from young men somewhere
else in the house. A fiddle is playing.*

*JHON and SHANK, each dressed only in a towel, are seated
on a wooden bench. It's hot.*

SHANK. All my life, I've nursed a horror of destitution. But it
isn't too bad at all. It's fun.

JHON. What kind of fun?

SHANK. It winks its eye. It leads me on. I wonder: what's
behind that door? Behind that face? I pulled a blanket from
a window. And the moon shone in and the midnight
beckoned. So I followed. Funny old place this is.

JHON. I'm used to it.

SHANK. Regular, are you?

JHON. Oh I am, I am. Anything you want to know, just ask.

SHANK. Who comes here?

JHON. Same old crowd as always. Buggers and sods.

SHANK. Are buggers and sods the same?

JHON. Strictly speaking, men are buggers and lads are sods.

SHANK. I thought that sods were cool and sly and buggers
were hot and lustful and covered in body-hair.

JHON. Well now you know. And boys are bumboys.

SHANK. Not in my house they aren't. My boys are decent. I was a bumboy.

JHON. I don't remember that.

SHANK. You were too busy to notice, chum. Don't get me started. I was a red-hot bumboy. Toast of the town. Some old looney wrote a pamphlet about me. They used to hand it out in the street. 'The playhouse youth with wild, lascivious limbs doth Satan's task perform.' Best fucking write-up I ever had. What's Honey?

JHON. Honey's a bedizened old whore of eighteen.

SHANK. I thought Honey was a Ganymede.

JHON. Ganymede's mother. What are you?

SHANK. I'm nothing, mate. Haven't the time. I've got my little actors to look after.

JHON. Don't you miss it?

SHANK. I find it less depressing missing it than having it.

JHON. Sad old fucker you are. Let's have some steam.

He ladles water on the brazier. Steam billows up.

I say, I'm sorry about that donkey business.

SHANK. Oh who cares.

JHON. My hands are tied. It's all new systems now. I hate it. It's like working in a factory. Somebody said you yelled at Dickie about the board.

SHANK. I did.

JHON. Well done, mate. 'Cause there's nobody else will speak their mind.

SHANK. I know there isn't, because they're fucking actors. All the guts of a feather bolster.

JHON. Do you know why the board is called a board?

SHANK. No?

JHON. It's because of those things you act on.

SHANK. Board? Oh, boards. Are you sure about that?

JHON. Oh yes. Quite sure. Because the original board had only got actors on it. There was Richard Burbage, Tommy Pope, Augustine Phillips . . .

SHANK. I was there, remember?

JHON. And the only one of all those bastards I remember with any respect is William Shakespeare.

SHANK. Oh really? What's his claim to fame?

JHON. He was the only one who didn't leave his shares to his wife and family.

SHANK. Only because he couldn't stand them. If he'd . . .

JHON. Ssh! There's someone coming.

The door creaks open and BLAGRAVE *comes in, wrapped in a towel. He takes a place on the bench, not recognising the others.* JHON *raises his eyebrows meaningfully at* SHANK. *After a moment:*

JHON. Quiet tonight, sir.

BLAGRAVE *ignores him.*

It's Jhon, sir. Jhon the dresser at the theatre. And Master Shank.

BLAGRAVE *recognises them.*

BLAGRAVE. Shank, I didn't expect to find you here. It's my first visit. Doctor's orders. But you mustn't let me interrupt you.

JHON. We were raking up the past, sir. Weren't we, Shanky? 'The playhouse youth . . . '. How does it go?

SHANK (*to* BLAGRAVE). One of my first successes. But I couldn't repeat it here.

BLAGRAVE. Ah yes, the years roll by and the memory fails.

JHON. Not mine, sir. I can remember lines from half a century back.

BLAGRAVE. Whose lines are they?

JHON. My own, sir. I wasn't always a dresser.

SHANK. Jhon was famous.

JHON. Oh I was, I was. I've been dreaming about it lately. I'm back on stage, I'm in my farthingale, I'm thrown a cue and blow me if it doesn't all come spouting out.

SHANK. Show us a bit.

JHON. Oh shut up, Shanky.

BLAGRAVE. Could you?

JHON. I *could* at the drop of a hat, sir. But I feel it isn't my place. Though . . .

He looks at them both.

. . . seeing as towels and steam are mighty levellers . . .

SHANK (*to* BLAGRAVE). I think we've hooked him. Rare occasion. (*To* JHON.) What will it be?

JHON. Oh, anything, mate. You cue me in.

SHANK. Um . . .

Bass voice:

'How can you fancy . . . ?'

JHON. Yes, I've got it. On you go.

SHANK. 'How can you fancy one that looks so fierce . . . ?' (*To* BLAGRAVE.) I'm a Mongol warrior.

JHON. Get on with it.

SHANK. 'Who, when he shall embrace you in his arms,
Will something forth his tales of war and blood,
Too harsh a subject for Zenocrate?'

*JHON replies. Through his dried-up voice and archaic style,
something thrilling and beautiful can be glimpsed. Slow
pace.*

JHON. 'As looks the sun through Nilus' flowing stream,
Or when the morning holds him in her arms,
So looks my lordly love, fair Tamburlaine;
His talk much sweeter than the Muses' song,
They sang for honour 'gainst Pierides,
Or when Minerva did with Neptune strive

For who was most mellifluous in their sound.
Whose eyes are brighter than the lamps of heaven,
Whose smile more radiant than the beams of dawn;
Who with his looks can'st clear the darkening sky,
And calm the rage of thundering Jupiter;
And higher would I raise my estimate
Than mighty Juno, when she . . . '

Pause.

Don't tell me.

Pause.

No, it's gone.

SHANK *applauds lightly.*

SHANK. Well done, Jhonno.

JHON. I was twenty-one when I played that, I was the oldest
leading lady in history.

SHANK. No you weren't.

JHON. I was!

SHANK. What about Johnny Thompson?

JHON. Oh my Lord, I'd blotted him out. He caused a riot. He
played the Duchess of Malfi with his wife and two nippers
in the audience, and one of 'em yelled out, 'Stop! Stop!
They're killing my dad!' (*To* BLAGRAVE.) It's just like
now, sir. No new boys. They can't be found. Dick Gunnell
tried his luck and look what happened to him.

BLAGRAVE. What do you mean?

JHON. Haven't you heard, sir? Poor old Dick's gone bankrupt.
And his lads all scattered.

BLAGRAVE *nods.*

BLAGRAVE. A theatre closed. A light gone out. And then they
wonder why the arts need supervision.

JHON. Very true, sir.

BLAGRAVE. The actor's gift is not a practical one. If he's left
to his own devices, then he'll spend more money than he
has in his purse, and go the way of Master Gunnell. Or he'll

stage some scandalous play which gives his enemies cause to close his theatre down. I love the theatre. I restrain its actors to protect its actors. That they resist my efforts is an eloquent witness to their innocence of the world.

He rises.

I shall not tell Sir Henry where I heard this news. I shall expect the same discretion from yourselves. (*To* JHON.) I enjoyed the memory. While it lasted. Good night to you both.

SHANK. Good night.

JHON. Good night, sir.

He goes.

Patronising bastard.

SHANK. Washes off my back, mate. Oh, I never got round to asking. What are you?

JHON. Bugger or sod, you mean? Well, nothing fits. So I've invented something new.

SHANK. What's that?

JHON. Bearing in mind my age, and some of the parts I've played, I've decided to call myself an old queen.

SHANK. I think that suits you very nicely, Jhonno.

JHON. Oh it does, it does. I'll tell you something else. I'm not the only one. There's more of us all the time.

End of scene.

Scene Six

Darkness. A sliver of light, and STEPHEN *emerges through a trapdoor, carrying a lighted candle. He looks down.*

STEPHEN. Come on up.

He stretches out a hand to help. HONEY *appears, also carrying a candle. The room gets lighter. It's the costume-store of* GUNNELL's *theatre, now seemingly stripped bare.*

Well?

HONEY. Where are we?

STEPHEN. We're in Master Gunnell's theatre.

HONEY. Where's the stage?

STEPHEN. Down there. We can look at it later, if you like. This is the costume-store. It's where I sleep. No, slept. Until today. We used to go out at night, exploring. Down that ladder, through the tunnel, into the stables and out into the alleyway. Sit down. I want you properly placed.

HONEY. What for?

STEPHEN. You'll see.

He sees a box.

This will do. Bit dusty.

He takes out his handkerchief and puts it over the box.

There.

HONEY. I think I'd rather sit on the dust.

STEPHEN. I see what you mean.

He dusts the box with his handkerchief.

You ready?

HONEY. Ready for what?

STEPHEN. I'll show you.

He pulls aside a curtain. We see three gowns hanging up. They're woven with metallic thread. They glitter in the candle-light.

Look.

He removes a gown, holds it up.

It's blended silk and wool. The silk is French, from Lyon. Those threads are gold.

He shows HONEY *the gown.*

Feel it.

HONEY *does.*

What do you think it's worth?

HONEY. I don't know.

STEPHEN. Guess.

HONEY. Five pounds?

STEPHEN. Five pounds! You can't be serious. This comes at seven and six a yard.

HONEY. Are they all like this?

STEPHEN. Like this or better. There's easily sixty poundsworth here. Hold it. See how heavy it is.

HONEY *takes it.*

Don't look so guilty. It can't be wrong to take them if we give them to Master Shank. Why don't you try it on?

HONEY. What for?

STEPHEN. I feel I ought to be making you comfortable. Go on. Just see if it fits.

HONEY *tries his hand in a sleeve of the gown.* STEPHEN *helps him.* HONEY *takes off his top and steps into the gown. It fits and looks good. It's a Caroline costume, less formal than the theatre costumes seen so far.*

It's a softer line than you normally wear. More natural, somehow. Take a few steps.

HONEY *takes a few steps in the gown.*

You see? It's loose. It swings about. It ought to look as though you threw it on casually while you were thinking about something more important. Do you want to smoke?

HONEY. Have you got anything?

STEPHEN. There might be a little something hidden away. Rough lot, those boys were. Shall I forage?

HONEY. Yes, if you like.

STEPHEN. Sit down then.

HONEY *sits.*

STEPHEN. It's strange being in a place you used to live in, when it's quiet and empty. That's where I used to sit and think. This is the bit of floor I slept on. Me, then Joshua, Samuel, Job, like books in the Bible. That's the cupboard Samuel locked me up in. I seem to bring out the worst in people.

HONEY. I thought you were going to forage.

STEPHEN. Abracadabra!

Without moving from the spot he's standing on, he presses a floorboard with his foot. It see-saws up, revealing a small cache below. He crouches, stretches a hand inside.

This was Job's. I've waited ages for a suitable chance to rob it.

Feels the tobacco.

Yes, it's here. And the pipe as well.

He takes out a wrapped twist of tobacco and a pipe. HONEY *reaches for it.* STEPHEN *holds it out of reach.*

No! I'm the host.

He sits on the floor, starts filling the pipe. It involves shredding the leaves and who knows what else. Lighting it is done with a flint from his pocket. Meanwhile:

Are you nervous about tomorrow?

HONEY. No.

STEPHEN. Nor me. I'm feeling thoroughly cool and calm. I've seen the play four times. You were always Titania except for once when you'd twisted your ankle. Richard Sharpe went on for you, and he was beneath contempt. You play her wonderfully. Last time you said 'But she, being mortal, of that child did die,' I thought my heart would break, it was so sad. But can I ask you a question?

HONEY *shrugs.*

Why do you wear such heavy paint?

HONEY. It doesn't look heavy onstage.

STEPHEN. I *mean* onstage. It doesn't look real. It's cakey. If you're worried about your beard, why don't you simply dust it with a little light powder? That would cover it. And your wig's too stiff, it looks like cardboard. You ought to tease it out with the end of a comb. I could show you, if you like.

HONEY. Don't bother.

STEPHEN. Well it was just a thought.

He lights the pipe, pulls it out of his mouth the moment it takes.

Here.

HONEY *takes it. Inhales deeply, closes his eyes, holds his breath.*

What's it like?

HONEY. It's good.

STEPHEN. Does it take long to work?

HONEY. No, it's immediate.

He inhales again.

STEPHEN. Is it working now?

HONEY. Mm hm.

STEPHEN. I tried it once but it didn't have the slightest effect on me.

He watches while HONEY *smokes.*

Old Shanky says that acting's all a matter of standing straight and saying your lines on cue. That isn't what he did, when he was young, I'd bet my life on it. It isn't what you do either. Is it?

After a moment:

HONEY. It's different at different times.

STEPHEN. How?

HONEY. Well, when you're young, you're just a child being clever. Then it changes.

STEPHEN. When?

HONEY. When you get older. When other boys get tall and clumsy. And their voices drop two million pegs. We don't do that. We hang on.

STEPHEN. What do you mean, hang on?

HONEY. I don't know. We just do. It's like a baby falling down a well. You've got its foot in your hand and you don't let go. So you're not one thing exactly. You're half man, half boy. That's when you find you can really do it. And it's amazing. It's better than beer or wine. It's better than smoking. It's like flying. It's like finding that wings have suddenly sprouted from your shoulders. You come on stage and everything happens the way it's meant to. And nobody in the audience looks at anyone else. Because you live in a sort of stolen time that they can't get to. Except through you. And it could disappear at any moment. You're like a soldier on the eve of battle. Every night could be your last. And everyone wants to be that special person on that special night. That's my theory. That's why they grab old Jhon, J, H, O, N, and give him notes for us. It's why they hang about at the Actors' Door.

He puts out the pipe, starts getting out of his dress.

I still get letters every day. Not just from men. Everyone thinks I'm just a boyish bugger. That's not true. I see women as well. They're even stranger than the men are. They ask me to supper and want me to bring my gown and make-up.

He stands, the gown in his arms.

Take it.

STEPHEN *takes it.* HONEY *gets the other gowns.*

We'll carry them back to Shanky. He'll pay his debt to the Board and you'll stay on. Isn't that what you wanted?

There's a loud knock downstairs.

Who's that?

STEPHEN. It must be Gunnell. Quick! Through there!

They blow out the candles and hide. After a moment, BLAGRAVE appears through the trapdoor, wrapped up for the night and carrying a lantern. He climbs in. Peers around.

BLAGRAVE. Hello? Hello? Master Gunnell?

He sniffs the air: Tobacco.

I know you're here.

He looks around. He looks at the costumes. Inspects them with appreciation. Feels the fabric of one. A moment's thought and then he bundles all three gowns into his arms. He picks up his lantern and goes, taking the gowns with him.

STEPHEN *and* HONEY *peer out from their hiding-place.*

STEPHEN. That wasn't Gunnell.

HONEY. That was Master Blagrave.

STEPHEN. Who's he?

HONEY. Someone very important.

He looks round.

Oh my God!

STEPHEN. What?

HONEY. He's taken the gowns!

STEPHEN *looks round.*

STEPHEN. I don't believe it!

He sits and buries his head in his hands.

HONEY. Shanky will have to sell you after all.

STEPHEN *looks up.*

STEPHEN. He won't. Do you really not know what I did today? Did you honestly think that Master Gunnell had sent me with a message? Or that he'd promised me First Fairy? Of course he hadn't. I made it up. I made it all up. I couldn't believe that you all believed me.

Pause.

I woke up this morning. And the house was empty. And I remembered it was Tuesday, and that Master Shank would need his fairies. And everything fitted. Because all I wanted, was to be where you were. Right from the very first time I saw you act. I wanted to talk with you. And smoke, just like we did tonight. I wanted to ask you, why did Samuel lock me in the cupboard? Why am I funny? Why are people always getting rid of me?

Pause.

And now that I've got you, I won't be got rid of again. I won't allow it.

ACT TWO

Scene One

SHANK's *room. Three weeks later. Morning light. There's a bottle of wine on the table. Costumes and properties have gone. The room looks empty and depressing.*

SHANK *shows* ROBINSON *into the room.*

SHANK. Come in, come in. Fancy a drink?

ROBINSON. I will.

SHANK. Take a seat. This won't take long.

He goes to the door and shouts down.

Master Honey! Will you come up here please?

He takes the bottle of wine. Knocks the waxen seal off the bottle, and will in time pour a drink for them both.

I keep this for the kids. They seem to like it. Sit down, you're making me nervous.

ROBINSON *sits.*

ROBINSON. I haven't been in this room for twenty years.

SHANK. Mm hm.

ROBINSON. It feels odd.

SHANK. You bet it does. It's bloody empty. Sold the lot, mate. Every property, every gown. As the pounds rolled in.

HONEY *appears in the doorway. He wears no shirt and his hair is plastered with what looks like mud.*

What have you done to your hair?

HONEY. I'm having it dyed.

SHANK. Dyed what?

HONEY. Dyed what it was. Before you made me look like Mouldy Meg the Sailor's Friend.

SHANK. Take this key.

He gives HONEY *the key from his belt.*

Go to my closet, open the safe and bring me the box.

HONEY. I thought you two were deadly enemies.

SHANK. We are.

HONEY. Why don't you show it?

SHANK. We will show it when we're ready. Don't presume to correct our timing. Off you go. Get one of the lads to help. It weighs a ton.

HONEY *goes out.*

(*Of the wine.*) What's it like?

ROBINSON. It's fine.

Pause.

How is your wife?

SHANK. She's well. She writes. She asks about you from time to time. Still calls you Curly.

ROBINSON. I was sitting at this table. Eating your stew. Making the same old jokes about it. You were studying your lines, over there by the fire. You laughed and said 'You'll never guess what the silly old bugger's done.' I came across and looked at it over your shoulder. And I saw my name in the script. At the top of a speech. 'The Devil is an Ass', Act Two, Scene Three.

He quotes:

'There's Dickey Robinson, a very pretty fellow . . . ' What came next?

SHANK. I don't remember.

ROBINSON *continues, faltering and leaving out the occasional word:*

ROBINSON. 'Dressed like a lawyer's wife, amongst them all,
(I lent him clothes) but, to see him behave it:
And lay the law: and carve; and drinke unto them;
Then talk bawdy, and send frolics! Oh!

It would have burst your buttons, or not left you
A seam.'

Pause.

It was the best.The best imaginable. But I can't remember it
now without it seeming shameful, somehow. Rotten. Like
that taste in your mouth when you're losing a tooth.

SHANK. Men who were bred from boys are damaged goods.

ROBINSON. Do you believe that?

SHANK. Fucking know it.

HONEY *and* STEPHEN *come in carrying a heavy box.*
STEPHEN*'s sleeves are rolled up and his hands are dyed*
brown.

On the table. Gently.

They place it on the table

That's it. Out.

SHANK *finds a small key from around his neck. To*
HONEY*:*

And wash that muck out of your hair.

STEPHEN. He can't. It has to stay for an hour or it all goes
yellow.

He and HONEY *go, closing the door behind them.* SHANK
unlocks the box.

SHANK. He's driving me mad, that boy. It's like sharing your
house with Little Miss Muffett.

ROBINSON. I thought you were selling him.

SHANK. I've got no takers. Just can't shift the little bastard.
There was one fellow showed some modest interest. Then
he came to see 'The Amazon Queen.' Stephen had one line.
One line. 'I with this lance have slain one hundred Romans.'
Well, they rocked. They shrieked. And that was the last I
heard of that suggestion.

The box is open.

Take a look.

ROBINSON *looks at it.*

ROBINSON. That's it?

SHANK. That's it.

ROBINSON. Five hundred pounds?

SHANK. As near as dammit.

ROBINSON. What do you . . . ?

SHANK. What you are looking at is four hundred and twenty-nine pounds, seventeen shillings and sixpence.

ROBINSON. Leaving . . .

SHANK. Seventy pounds and half a crown.

ROBINSON. When do I get it?

SHANK. You don't.

ROBINSON. But you said . . .

SHANK. Jesus, Dickie, what do you want? I've nothing left. Honey's a scrag-end. Goffe is Goffe.

ROBINSON. What about Trigg?

SHANK. I've had no offers.

ROBINSON. Tommy Pollard wants to buy him.

SHANK. Tommy, eh? That's a turn-up. Tommy was one of my lads. Horrible nasty nature. Hit his father.

ROBINSON. *He* did?

SHANK. I did. Decked the bastard. Oh we were reckless spirits in those days, matey. Cannikins clinking. Fine display of self-indulgent bollocks. What's Tommy offering?

ROBINSON. Twenty.

SHANK. Tell him to fuck himself.

ROBINSON. What if he offers more?

SHANK. The same but louder. Sorry old chum. I'd rather go belly up.

ROBINSON. You are belly up. You owe seventy pounds and half a crown and you haven't got it.

SHANK. Mm.

Pause.

Prison, is it?

ROBINSON. Don't be ridiculous.

SHANK. Do I keep my job?

ROBINSON. Not on the same arrangement.

SHANK. Meaning what?

ROBINSON. We'll offer you parts. You can reject them or accept them as you please. It's called freelancing.

SHANK. I know what it's bloody well called, you liar. It's called the sack.

He stands.

From you. The boy I fed. The boy I taught. The boy I found in a poorhouse!

He bangs the table.

ROBINSON. You'd have been sacked five years ago if it wasn't for me. I protect you against the Board. I cover up for you. I go round the dressing-room, sick with embarrassment, saying, oh he was just a little bit off today, I'll talk to him. Knowing that when I do, you'll patronise me. As though I'm the one who's pissing on the magical fucking flame.

SHANK. Oh, let's not quarrel, old dear. Not now. I'm through.

Pause.

I was close. So close. I nearly did it. Little Stephen made a raid on Gunnell's. He found three gowns worth seventy, eighty pounds. And he was just on the point of bringing them back when something happened so mysterious . . . shocking almost . . . that try as I might I cannot understand it. Blagrave arrived and stole them.

ROBINSON. No he didn't.

SHANK. I've got witnesses.

ROBINSON. He confiscated them. And then he bought them.

SHANK. Why? What for? It isn't even as though they'd fit him.

ROBINSON. He's going to run a theatre.

SHANK. Blagrave? When does he plan to open?

ROBINSON. Christmas.

SHANK. Where?

ROBINSON. He's buying Gunnell's.

SHANK *laughs.*

SHANK. Ha ha! You're fucked.

ROBINSON. We are.

SHANK. Deeply, painfully.

ROBINSON. Face in the bolster.

SHANK. Face in the fucking floorboards. Oh I'll laugh. You'll hear me hooting. From my little square of gutter. Let me give you an example.

He laughs. Pours more wine for them both.

You might find a play. Some thrilling, wonderful play. On a topical subject. Witches. No, *a* witch. With one big part for a character actor. And he'll say, oh no, you cannot perform that play because there *are* no witches. Or, there are lots of witches but they're witches. Then *he'll* do the witchy play, and you'll have to do 'The Coursing of a Hare, or The Madcap'.

He laughs. They drink.

ROBINSON. Why don't you sell him Stephen?

SHANK. Mmh. Nice thought. I might get ten. Although it's more than the lad is worth.

ROBINSON. You might get more. If we presented Stephen. If we served him up onstage with all the trimmings.

SHANK. What would he play?

ROBINSON. Oh . . . Something showy.

SHANK. Not an Amazon.

ROBINSON. Not an Amazon, no.

SHANK. And nothing with too many lines.

ROBINSON. Nothing with too many lines, but a title role.

SHANK. You serious?

ROBINSON. Yes. I am. We'll get a new costume made. New wig. The Board will pay. And after the show you can name your price.

SHANK. Twenty? Thirty?

ROBINSON. What would you say to seventy pounds and half a crown?

SHANK. For Stephen?

ROBINSON. When I was his age, somebody tried to buy me for a hundred.

SHANK. He can't act.

ROBINSON. When I first played Olivia, I knew nothing. I didn't even know what acting was. I wore a very becoming bombazine mourning gown, a string of ebony beads and a jet tiara. And the rest was you. You'd taught me every gesture, every inflection, every move. The house went wild and the following morning I was famous.

SHANK. What's your name?

ROBINSON. I want you to do it again. I want you to make little Stephen Hammerton look like the best young actor that ever there was. And then we'll sell him off to Blagrave as his leading lady. After that, the worse he acts, the happier I shall be. He'll be our Trojan horse.

End of scene.

Scene Two

Later that week. The stage at the Globe. Morning. There's a painted tree onstage from the night before. SHANK's old work-bag stands on the floor.

ALEX *and* TRIGG *are sweeping the stage.* ALEX *stops, looks at the tree.*

ALEX. What most inspires the inner eye? Description or depiction?

TRIGG. I'm sweeping.

ALEX. When the eye is feasted, does the imagination starve?

TRIGG. I think I've got it. Ask me one last time.

ALEX. Are paint and canvas enemies to fancy?

TRIGG. Do you mean, have plays got too much scenery?

ALEX. Yes. And does it make the poetry less important?

TRIGG. There's no such thing as too much scenery. In winter, when we play indoors, we'll have whole palaces on stage. And woods and jungles. And stormy seas and clouds coming down with gods and goddesses bestowing bounty. I'd rather see that than any amount of acting.

HONEY *comes on.*

ALEX. Good morning.

HONEY. Morning.

TRIGG. Somebody didn't get home last night.

HONEY. Who's got my roll?

ALEX. It's there.

He indicates SHANK*'s bag.*

In Shanky's bag.

TRIGG. Dare we open it?

ALEX. You go first.

TRIGG *opens the bag and feels about inside.* HONEY *waits.*

TRIGG. This will be painful. Here.

He brings out a very small square of paper. Holds it up.

Here.

HONEY *stares at it.*

HONEY. That's it?

TRIGG *gives it to* HONEY.

TRIGG. That's it.

HONEY *counts his lines while the boys watch with macabre interest.*

(*To* ALEX.) One scene!

ALEX. What an insult.

TRIGG. She does get talked about a lot. You could say in a way it's almost flattering to be cast as Helen of Troy. Didn't she have the face that launched a thousand ships?

ALEX. That was when the war *began.* This is seven years later. She probably couldn't launch a leaky life-boat.

SHANK *comes on.* STEPHEN *follows him.*

SHANK (*to* ALEX *and* TRIGG). Pass my bag. (*To* HONEY, *of his roll.*) I see you've found it. (*To* ALEX *and* TRIGG.) Go to the wardrobe. Jhon is waiting.

ALEX *and* TRIGG *go, one of them passing* SHANK *his bag en route. To* STEPHEN:

Shoe.

He throws a shoe to STEPHEN *who catches it unathletically.*

(*To* HONEY.) Look at the way he catches. (*To* STEPHEN.) Shoe.

He throws the second shoe, with the same result.

Skirt.

He hands it over.

Change in the wings. Off you go.

STEPHEN *goes off-stage. To* HONEY:

Look at the way he walks. He's like a cat with rickets. I don't know why I agreed to this. I'm terrified. I couldn't get out of bed this morning.

HONEY. I couldn't get out fast enough.

SHANK. Whose bed was that?

HONEY. Never you mind. I'm depressed.

SHANK. We're both depressed.

HONEY. I'm five foot nine. And that's in stockings. Hardly anyone likes my acting. Nobody under forty even likes my body.

SHANK. It gets worse.

HONEY. It *has* got worse. (*Of his roll.*) Seventeen lines. And they're rubbish.

He reads in a silly voice:

'Dear Lord, you are full of fair words.'

He does a tinkling laugh down the scale.

Witty, eh? Here's a very good speech. 'Oh sir – .' That's it. 'Oh sir – .' How do I play it. Mm? Disdainful?

'Oh sir – '? Coquettish? 'Oh sir – .' For vulgar comedy?

SHANK. Enough, enough. Now listen. This is secret. He'll play once. And then we'll sell him. That is the plan. Your position is utterly different. You have months and months to go. Your crowning months. Vittoria Corombona. Gertrude. Now hurry him up.

HONEY *goes.* SHANK *waits. He's edgy and nervous.* STEPHEN *comes on in skirt and women's shoes.*

STEPHEN. Honey's upset.

SHANK. That's not upset. When Master Robinson lost Boadicea to Tommy Holcombe, he burnt his chariot.

He indicates a place onstage.

Go there.

STEPHEN. I don't know why you're making me do this. I think it's mad. Couldn't I just play a waiting-woman?

SHANK. What makes you think that you could play a waiting-woman?

STEPHEN. I wouldn't have to act. I'd just be standing.

SHANK. Show me how you stand.

STEPHEN stands.

STEPHEN. Oh I forgot. Feet.

He puts his feet apart.

It doesn't make it any easier, your scowling like that.

Tries standing as he's been told.

How's this?

SHANK. We'll look at it as we go.

Pause.

STEPHEN. What are we going to do?

SHANK. I'm thinking.

He looks around the stage, with little idea of where to start.

Look at the stage.

STEPHEN. I've seen it.

SHANK. Look again.

STEPHEN. What for?

SHANK. It's what I do when I first come into a theatre. Move up a little. No, up. Up! That's it. That's the spot.

STEPHEN. Why's this the spot?

SHANK. You'll see in a minute. Now look. No, look around you. Far as you can. What's the throw?

STEPHEN. The what?

SHANK. The throw.

STEPHEN. What's that?

SHANK. It's what I look for. Where I'll pitch my voice. The wall at the back, the upper levels. And the audience. There.

He directs STEPHEN's gaze to the left, then to the centre, then to the right.

And there. And there. They're on three sides. Those below you will support you. If you show them who's in charge. As you go up, they get more testing. There. And there.

He takes up position.

This is the spot. It used to be known as Shanky's spot. Watch what I do.

He speaks the speech with pathos:

'I have had a dream, past the wit of man to say what dream it was: man is but an ass, if he go about to expound this dream.' Now watch.

He includes all the house:

'Methought I was – there is no man can tell what. Methought I was – and methought I had – but man is but a patched fool if he will offer to say what methought I had. The eye of man hath not heard . . . ' You see? Now listen.

They listen to the low murmur from outside.

The sound of London. Carts, cries, boatmen. Don't try to shout above it. It's bigger than you. Cut into it.

He raises his voice.

Hey! Now you.

STEPHEN. Hey.

SHANK. Louder.

STEPHEN. Hey!

SHANK. More.

STEPHEN. Hey!

SHANK. Don't shout.

STEPHEN. Hey!

SHANK. Sharper.

STEPHEN. Hey!

SHANK. Good. Better. Give me your roll.

STEPHEN *does.*

STEPHEN. It's old.

SHANK *looks at the roll.*

SHANK. It is.

He looks at the roll. Crackles it, smells it.

This was copied for the first performance. Henry? Harry. Harry. He was the good one. Harry, half-blind, stuck in a corner, warming his toes at a fire. And every so often, the flames shot up as he fed them a page. Here's a correction.

Squints at it. STEPHEN *looks.*

STEPHEN. Who wrote it?

SHANK *looks.*

SHANK. The poet.

He looks at the correction.

No, we'll keep it as it was.

STEPHEN (*points*). Who wrote that?

SHANK. That is the actor's note. Salamon Pavy. When he was nervous he would nibble the corners

He shows STEPHEN.

STEPHEN. Was he the boy who died?

SHANK. He was. Although his death was unconnected.

STEPHEN. What was it not connected with?

SHANK *examines the roll.*

If it was unconnected, then there must have been a thing or time or story . . .

SHANK. He was cast as Cressida. But he lost the part. Because he didn't know it at the run-through. Take your place.

STEPHEN *does. Waits.*

It was his second scene.

He finds the place in the roll.

We were rehearsing in the Middle Temple. Which has an echo. So the silence when he stopped was all the more . . . foreboding. He got a prompt. Which meant a whack that evening. That was the way we worked in those days. Then another. On it went. And then a long, long silence. I closed my eyes, and when I opened them again, he was crying.

Spouts of water shooting out of his eyes, horizontally, like a nursery-picture. Somebody beckoned. And I stepped forward.

STEPHEN. Did you play the part?

SHANK. I did. And I was highly praised.

He shows STEPHEN *a section of the roll, his hand placed to cover what follows.*

Go from here.

STEPHEN *goes into place. Stands.*

Legs!

STEPHEN *adjusts his stance.* SHANK *marks the cue:*

SHANK. 'As true as Troilus' shall crown up the verse,
And sanctify the numbers.'

STEPHEN *starts. He's nervous and gauche and directs the lines to* SHANK. SHANK *mostly reads the roll.*

STEPHEN. 'Prophet may you be!
If I be false or swerve a hair from truth,
When time is old and hath forgot itself,
When waterdrops have worn the stones of Troy,
And blind oblivion swallowed cities up,
And mighty states characterless are grated
To dusty nothing; yet let memory,
From false to false, among young maids in love . . . '

He awkwardly raises both hands, palms forward.

' . . . Upbraid my falsehood!'

SHANK *looks up with interest.*

SHANK. What's that?

STEPHEN. What's what?

SHANK. The gesture.

STEPHEN. Did you like it?

SHANK. No I didn't. But it caught my attention, which is more than I can say for anything else you've done so far. What was it?

STEPHEN. It was 'Assevero', sir. To swear.

SHANK. From John Bulwer's 'Rules of Rhetoric'?

STEPHEN. Yes, sir. Page four, sir.

SHANK. I know the page. Who taught you that?

STEPHEN. Master Gunnell.

SHANK. Did he indeed. How many gestures did he teach you?

STEPHEN. All two hundred.

SHANK. The poor old bugger. Nobody's done that stuff on stage for twenty years. Show me another. Show me 'Dolebit'.

STEPHEN *does a formal gesture of supplication: hands clasped before him.*

Show me 'Inventione labora'.

STEPHEN *puts tip of right forefinger against his lips: a musing gesture, faintly ridiculous.*

Start again. Start with 'Exclamationem aptat'. That's what I did.

Pause.

Go on.

STEPHEN. It doesn't feel right, sir. Doing a gesture out of a book. I only did it before because I thought you'd want it. But if nobody does it any longer . . . ?

SHANK. Have you finished?

STEPHEN. Yes, sir.

SHANK. The reason nobody does it any longer, is that they've forgotten the meaning. Try it. Then I'll show you.

STEPHEN *raises a hand, thumb and fingers apart.*

STEPHEN. 'Prophet may you . . . !'

SHANK. Drop your shoulders.

STEPHEN *tries again.*

STEPHEN. 'Prophet may you . . . !'

SHANK. The hand goes further up.

STEPHEN *tries again.*

STEPHEN. 'Prophet may you be . . . !'

SHANK. Stop.

STEPHEN. What's wrong?

SHANK. I'm thinking.

Pause.

You have to follow it with your body. As though you'd never done it before. As though *no-one* had done it before. I can't explain. Start when I clap my hands.

STEPHEN *waits. Tenses.*

Drop your shoulders. Good. Now think about something else.

He relaxes, looks around as though uninvolved and not about to clap at all.

Look at those leaves.

He claps unexpectedly. STEPHEN *springs into action: raises his hand and speaks with some passion.*

STEPHEN. 'Prophet may you be . . . !'

SHANK. And drop.

STEPHEN *drops his hand arbitrarily.*

No, find the *meaning*. Do it like this.

He raises his hand, palm outwards, then starts the speech, lowering his hand very slowly. It's beautiful, strange: a bit Kabuki but full of emotion. He's rapt and youthful. In contrast to the slowness of his gestures, his speech is quick and light.

'Prophet may you be!
If I be false, or swerve a hair from truth,
When time is old and hath forgot itself,
When waterdrops have worn the stones of Troy, . . . '

Slowly he raises the other hand, then raises both hands very slowly, palms outwards. Meanwhile:

' . . . And blind oblivion swallowed cities up,
And mighty states characterless are grated
To dusty nothing . . . '
Now it's 'assevero'!

Slowly, he raises both hands higher till they reach arms-length. Meanwhile:

' . . . yet let memory,
From false to false, among false maids in love,
Upbraid my falsehood . . . !'

He has reached a peak of enormous energy, his whole body thrown into the gesture. Now he modulates the gesture into one which eventually will come to rest with one hand on his heart. Meanwhile:

Now tilt the body.

Tilts his body.

'When they've said, 'As false,
As air, as water, wind or sandy earth . . . '
Now see each one.

He very lightly differentiates the different creatures:

'As fox to lamb, as wolf to heifer's calf,
Pard to the hind, or stepdame to her son' –
And up . . .

He starts to raise one hand to the opening position:

'Yea, let them say, to something something falsehood,
As false as Cressid.'

He stops, one hand raised.

That was shit.

STEPHEN. It wasn't.

SHANK. Not entirely. There aren't a lot of us left. Go back to the start. The start was good.

STEPHEN. It just came out.

SHANK. That's why it was good. You have to say each word as though it had sprung into your mind that very moment. If you don't, I'll stop you. And I'll stop you when I don't believe you. And I'll stop you when you gabble. I'll stop you when you fail to taste each word as though it were the first apple of the year. I'll stop you when you hunch your shoulders up, and by Christ I'll stop you when you toss your head and flutter your eyelids. It will be hard. You'll

cry. And then I'll make you do it again. And you'll be
better. We'll work all morning and we'll work till midnight.
And you'll dream about it. And you'll think about it every
waking moment till they're putting you into your gown.
And then you'll think of nothing but your face and wig
and the party afterwards. And you'll be good. You'll be as
good as Honey. You'll be better. You'll be as good as Master
Robinson was. And he was good. I am the only man in
England who can make that promise. Start again.

STEPHEN. What's the point? If all you're doing is selling me
off to Master Blagrave?

SHANK. Did Honey tell you that?

STEPHEN *nods.*

SHANK. A little story. When Queen Elizabeth was old, she
would allow no looking-glasses near her. A man was
employed to paint her face, and when she annoyed him,
which was often, he would colour her nose bright red. She
used to totter around all day wondering why her courtiers
were in fits of laughter. If you stay in theatre, which I hope
you will, you'll find this tale a very useful metaphor for the
kind of advice one tends to get from one's fellow-actors.
Excellent boys are never got rid of. Never. If you are good,
you'll stay. Now start.

STEPHEN *stands ready.*

Chest out.

STEPHEN *begins.*

STEPHEN. 'Prophet may you be . . . '

SHANK. He's there.

He indicates a spot on the stage. STEPHEN *starts again,
addressing the imaginary Troilus.*

STEPHEN. 'Prophet may you be!'

If *I* be *false . . . '*

SHANK. In English. '*If* I be *false . . . '*

STEPHEN. '*If* I be false, or swerve a hair from truth . . . '

SHANK. Don't rush.

STEPHEN. '*If* I be false, or swerve a hair from truth . . . '

SHANK. From *what*?

STEPHEN. From truth.

SHANK. From *what?*

STEPHEN. Truth.

SHANK. Can't hear you.

STEPHEN. *Truth. Truth. Truth.*

SHANK. Say it.

STEPHEN. 'If I be false, or swerve a hair from truth . . . '

SHANK. Breathe.

STEPHEN. I don't need to.

SHANK. *Breathe.*

STEPHEN. 'If I be false, or swerve a hair from truth . . . '

SHANK *gestures:* STEPHEN, *responding, breathes and modulates:*

'When time is old and hath forgot itself,
When waterdrops have worn the stones of Troy . . . '

SHANK (*shouts*). Of where?

STEPHEN (*shouts*). Of Troy!

SHANK (*shouts*). Say it! ' . . . stones of Troy/And blind oblivion . . . '

STEPHEN *joins in:*

STEPHEN. 'And blind oblivion swallowed cities up . . . '

SHANK. And breathe and . . .

STEPHEN. 'And mighty states characterless are grated.

To dusty nothing . . . '

SHANK. Run on. 'Grated to dusty . . . '

STEPHEN. 'And mighty states characterless are grated
To dusty nothing . . . '

SHANK. Go up.

STEPHEN. ' . . . to dusty nothing . . . '

SHANK. Up. There's more to come. ' . . . to dusty nothing . . . '

STEPHEN. 'To dusty nothing, yet let memory . . . '

SHANK. Better.

STEPHEN. ' . . . From false to false . . . '

SHANK. Change key.

STEPHEN. ' . . . among young maids in love . . .

He raises his hands.

. . . upbraid my . . . '

SHANK. Stop. I didn't believe it. Start again.

End of scene.

Scene Three

Rousing applause is heard: it's the curtain-call.

As it fades, we see the dining-hall of an eating-house frequented by theatricals. Large table. A couple of bottles of wine, pre-ordered. JHON is seated. ROBINSON comes in. He's only just come off-stage, and still wears vestiges of make-up.

JHON. Good evening, Master Robinson. We're the first. I took this chair. I hope it's not the wrong one. But it's tricky on these occasions. There's people who say they'll come, who don't. And those who say they won't, who bring their aunts and uncles.

ROBINSON. How did you think it went?

JHON. Oh smooth, quite smooth. They're always heavyish on the wardrobe, sir, these plays with opposite armies. It's all those armbands.

SHANK appears.

There's Master Shank. Oh dear, oh dear. I hear he's very upset.

SHANK *arrives at the table.*

SHANK. I shan't be staying.

JHON. Oh, sit down anyway, Shanky Anyone mind if I do the honours?

SHANK *sits heavily.* JHON *pours him a drink.*

SHANK. Thank you, Jhonno. Christ, I need it. (*To* ROBINSON.) Go on. Say it. I'm a failure. I'm a fallen fucking Titan.

JHON. Oh it's only another show.

SHANK (*to* ROBINSON). I wish you'd seen him in rehearsal.

ROBINSON. What was he like?

SHANK. Not bad. Quite good in the last few days. He got a bit nervous at the run-through. So I bollocked him. Maybe I got it wrong. Oh I don't know. I never imagined *this* would happen. Blimey.

ROBINSON. He said the lines.

SHANK. I wished he hadn't.

ROBINSON. They heard him.

SHANK. Oh, they heard him.

ROBINSON. He even got some laughs I hadn't expected.

SHANK. That was *at* him. *I'd* get laughs if I carried on like that. So would you. So would the theatre cat. Where's that bottle?

ROBINSON *pours wine.* SHANK *drinks.*

I knew he'd gone all wrong from the moment he walked on stage. With one hip up. And the other one tracing hieroglyphics in the air. He wriggled his arse. He batted his eyelids. Pouted. And that kissing scene . . . ! Jesus! I had to avert my eyes. I blushed. I was the first Pandarus in history to be visibly shocked.

ROBINSON (*to* JHON). What did *you* think?

JHON. Not to my taste at all, sir. I do hope it won't be catching on. It's the influence on the younger lads I worry about.

All sit gloomily. At last, with caution:

Although I did hear tell that Master Benfield's mother liked him.

Bemused pause.

SHANK. Dotty, is she?

JHON. No she isn't. She's my Friday night shove ha'penny partner.

ROBINSON. Does she visit the theatre often?

JHON. That's the curious thing, sir. All the time. A most reliable lady.

BLAGRAVE *is there.*

BLAGRAVE. Good evening, Master Robinson.

ROBINSON. Master Blagrave. Won't you join us?

BLAGRAVE. Briefly, briefly.

He sits. The others exchange glances, trying to gauge his reaction.

Nobody told me that Sir Henry would be in the audience. I must attend his carriage. Good evening, Master Shank. We have a conversation pending, do we not, about the Cressida boy? Later, perhaps, we might discuss it. Or tomorrow.

SHANK *takes this as unequivocal thumbs-down.*

SHANK. Or tomorrow.

BLAGRAVE. Master Robinson, that was a sensitive portrayal.

ROBINSON. Thank you.

BLAGRAVE. Was it *too* sensitive I wonder? Hector, to my eye, is a portrait in oils. Whereas you depicted him in water-colours.

ROBINSON. Thank you. Useful note.

BLAGRAVE. Shank, I found you funny but excessive. It was the giggle. And the all-too-frequent rubbing of the hands. I felt that you were telling us what you *thought* of panders.

ROBINSON. Did Sir Henry feel that . . .

SHANK. What makes you think that you can run a theatre?

ROBINSON (*very quietly*). Shut up, Shanky.

BLAGRAVE. What a curious question. I've seen a thousand plays. I've read the accounts of every London playhouse. I do not believe there is a man alive who has a better grasp of the essentials.

He drinks. This isn't his first glass, nor is he used to drinking.

SHANK. You see no ethical dilemma?

JHON and ROBINSON kick him under the table.
BLAGRAVE laughs pleasantly.

BLAGRAVE. None at all. I'll bring my civic influence and professional skills to the aid of a shipwrecked enterprise. What's wrong with that?

SHANK. Is that Sir Henry's view?

BLAGRAVE. Sir Henry says he'll sleep all the better for knowing that there's at least one theatre in London which isn't run by hysterics.

He laughs.

But I mustn't invade your first-performance party. We shall talk anon. (*To all.*) Good night.

ROBINSON. Good night.

He goes.

SHANK. 'Talk anon' didn't sound too bad.

JHON. I thought that too. I thought it quite encouraging.

ROBINSON. I'll get him back. Let me do the talking this time.

SHANK. Try for a fiver.

ROBINSON goes after BLAGRAVE. SHANK drinks, relaxes.

That's my shot, old shiner. No more boys.

JHON. You always say that.

SHANK. No, it's true this time. I'm giving it up. I'll rent a cottage. In the country. With a garden. Not that convoluted nonsense, hedges cut into birds and hippopotami. Normal flowers. Those tall ones. Hollyhocks. And lines of brassicas, all bright and green, because three times a day some nice fat lady comes out of the kitchen door and throws the washing-up water all over them. Hello lads.

TRIGG *and* ALEX *appear and take seats.*

TRIGG. One of the waiters thought that I was Stephen.

ALEX. He wanted Trigg to sign his apron.

TRIGG. Where's he gone?

ALEX. He must be smoking with the other waiters.

TRIGG. That's why they're always so excited.

ALEX. When you see them.

TRIGG. *If* you see them.

BLAGRAVE *appears with* ROBINSON.

ROBINSON. Sir Henry's vanished.

BLAGRAVE. Master Robinson has persuaded me to join your party.

ALEX. I'm starving.

ROBINSON. Wait for the others.

BLAGRAVE (*to* TRIGG). I'll sit here.

He sits next to TRIGG.

ROBINSON (*to* SHANK, *of* BLAGRAVE). You won't believe this. I think he liked him.

SHANK. What!

BLAGRAVE (*to* TRIGG). Fork on that side, spoon at the top.

ROBINSON. He wants to sign him up for his opening show.

BLAGRAVE (*to* TRIGG). Napkin there.

SHANK. Oh cheer me up. Make it a good one. What's it called?

ROBINSON. The play? It's called 'The Hungarian Lion'.

SHANK *dissolves in laughter;* ROBINSON *laughs too.*

BLAGRAVE. It would be nice to eat.

JHON. I can order for you, sir.

SHANK (*to* ROBINSON). Or what?

ROBINSON. What do you mean, 'or what'?

SHANK. It's got to be called 'The Hungarian Lion' or something else.

ROBINSON. He says he sees no need for an alternative.

SHANK. Neither do I, mate. That'll do.

They laugh even more.

JHON (*to* BLAGRAVE). All of them know me here.

SHANK. 'The Hungarian Lion'. I love it. Oh I love it.

JHON (*to* BLAGRAVE). There's grouse . . .

ROBINSON (*to* SHANK). I've asked for twenty.

SHANK. *Twenty!*

ALEX (*to* ROBINSON). One of the waiters wanted Trigg to sign his apron.

ROBINSON. Why?

TRIGG. He thought that I was Stephen.

ROBINSON. Nobody told me that.

JHON. There's turkey, cygnet . . .

ROBINSON (*to* ROBINSON). Don't have the turkey.

ALEX. And the cygnet tastes of mackerel.

ROBINSON. If I'd known about the waiter, I'd have asked for thirty.

HONEY *appears.*

TRIGG. Look, there's Honey.

ALEX/TRIGG. Over here! Here we are!

HONEY. Has anyone here seen Master Waverley?

JHON. Venison pie.

ROBINSON. Don't have the venison.

HONEY. Where do I sit?

ROBINSON. Don't have anything in a pie.

HONEY *takes a place.*

TRIGG. Master Honey likes the hotpot.

HONEY. I'm not staying.

JHON (*to* BLAGRAVE). We players have been attending in this eating-house since 1590. Since Master Alleyn first founded it. Old Edward, that was. Then young Thomas owned it for a couple of years. And now it's his grandson, Joe.

TRIGG. One doesn't exactly come here for the food.

JHON *continues to take and try to remember orders, ad lib. Meanwhile:*

ALEX. Honey says he's eating later.

BLAGRAVE (*to* TRIGG). That was a splendid showing, Master Trigg.

JHON (*to* BLAGRAVE). Boeuf en daube?

ALEX (*to* ROBINSON). Master Blagrave says that Trigg was splendid.

HONEY. All two speeches?

ROBINSON (*to* HONEY). What's happened to Stephen?

ALEX (*imitates* TRIGG). 'Sir, my Lord would instantly speak with you.'

ALEX,ROBINSON,HONEY,TRIGG. 'Where?'

ALEX (*and the others join in*). 'At your own house, there he unarms him!'

Applause.

HONEY (*to* ROBINSON). Stephen's talking to Sir Henry.

ROBINSON. Is he? Really? Did Sir Henry like him?

HONEY (*indicates Blagrave*). Ask *him.*

BLAGRAVE (*to* TRIGG). 'House' and comma. '*There*' he unarms him.'

ROBINSON. Well done Goffe!

TRIGG. Whose role from start to finish reads as follows:

ALEX, HONEY, ROBINSON, TRIGG. 'No sir, he stays for you to conduct him thither!'

Ironic cheers, applause and laughter.

BLAGRAVE. But is there not an ancient theatrical adage . . .

SHANK (*to* ROBINSON). Oh my Gawd, he's going native on us.

BLAGRAVE. 'There are no small parts, only small boys'.

He puts his hand matily on TRIGG*'s shoulder.*

TRIGG (*mutters*). 'O floorboards, ope and swallow me up.'

JHON (*tries to remember*). Turkey, cygnet, venison pie . . .

ROBINSON. Master Blagrave, have you seen Sir Henry?

BLAGRAVE. Not as yet. I'm so enjoying myself. Remind me: was the price of Stephen Hammertoii twenty pounds or guineas?

ROBINSON. It was guineas. But I don't believe we quite got round to agreeing the term.

BLAGRAVE. Surely we meant the term of his indenture?

TRIGG. Please can I have the 'Rabbit Surprize'?

ALEX. That's the 'Specialité de la maison'.

BLAGRAVE (*to* ALEX). What's that?

TRIGG. It's French.

ROBINSON (*quietly to* SHANK). I'll say two years.

BLAGRAVE. No, how do they serve it?

HONEY *is trying to get* ROBINSON*'s attention.*

HONEY. Dickie.

ALEX. Rabbit, boiled and the bones removed, stuffed with forcemeat, restored to rabbity shape, browned with a salamander and brought to the table with a bunch of myrtle in its mouth and its jawbones stuck in its eyes. That's what makes it so surprising.

TRIGG. For the rabbit.

HONEY. Dickie.

BLAGRAVE. But the recipe was well remembered. 'Rabbit boiled, and . . . '

He continues trying to remember, prompted by TRIGG *and* ALEX.

HONEY. Dickie, listen.

ROBINSON (*to* HONEY). What?

HONEY. They liked him.

ROBINSON. Who did?

HONEY. Who do you think?

ROBINSON. The audience?

HONEY. Yes the audience. They adored him. Next time give him a solo call.

ALEX (*to the table at large*). A test! A memory test!

TRIGG (*to all*). A test for Alex! Empty your pockets!

HONEY. Has anyone seen Master Waverley?

ALEX *closes his eyes till further notice. People empty their pockets with varying degrees of willingness. Some need prompting by* TRIGG, *and all report on the contents while putting them down on the table, ad lib. Meanwhile:*

ROBINSON (*to* BLAGRAVE). Six months.

HONEY (*to the table at large*). Has anyone seen here seen Master Waverley the brewer?

BLAGRAVE. Six months for twenty guineas? Can that really be correct?

HONEY. Portly person?

ROBINSON. No it isn't correct, exactly.

HONEY. Thanks for the help.

He goes out.

ROBINSON. What I meant was six months for seventy pounds and half a crown.

SHANK (*quietly to* ROBINSON). You're mad. You're raving.

BLAGRAVE. Might that include a non-compulsory option for a further year?

ROBINSON. I'll think about it.

BLAGRAVE (*to* TRIGG). Who is Master Waverley?

SHANK (*to* ROBINSON). Take it. Jump at it.

ROBINSON. I'm getting worried. It's too easy.

BLAGRAVE (*to* ROBINSON). Well?

ROBINSON. I'm thinking.

BLAGRAVE. Take your time.

JHON. I'm going to go round the table just once more.

BLAGRAVE (*to* TRIGG). Pass that bottle.

JHON. You lads will have to eat what's given you.

ROBINSON (*to* SHANK). First Bobby Benfield's mother liked him. Then the waiter with his apron. Then I talked to Honey.

BLAGRAVE. No, the red one.

SHANK. What did Honey have to say?

ROBINSON. He says the audience liked him too. He says we ought to give him a solo call.

JHON (*to* BLAGRAVE). What did you order, sir?

BLAGRAVE. A fillet of fish. Well-grilled.

ROBINSON. And one more bottle of each.

Hoorays and applause as STEPHEN *appears, accompanied by* HONEY. *They bring bottles. Applause, perhaps, from other unseen tables.*

TRIGG. Pride of place!

ALEX. Big chair!

HONEY. Look everyone! Lady Herbert has presented Stephen with her handkerchief.

He waves it. All cheer and the handkerchief is passed around.

BLAGRAVE. 'Lady Amelia' would be more correct.

TRIGG. Give us a look.

ALEX. It's all embroidered.

BLAGRAVE *rises to his feet and knocks on his glass with a spoon.*

BLAGRAVE. If I may . . .

ROBINSON (*to* SHANK). That's it. He's not for sale.

SHANK. What are you talking about?

ROBINSON. We can't afford to let him go. Not if Lady Amelia liked him.

SHANK. Jesus, Dickie! You're my friend! You cannot do this!

ALEX (*his eyes still closed*). What's that noise?

TRIGG. He's tapping a glass.

BLAGRAVE. If I may . . .

SEVERAL. Ssh.

TRIGG. Goffe's peeping.

ALEX (*who isn't*). I'm not!

ROBINSON. Quiet, you two.

SHANK (*to* ROBINSON). You treacherous bastard.

SEVERAL. Ssh!

JHON. Has anyone got a pencil?

SEVERAL. Ssh!

Silence.

BLAGRAVE. If I may 'wet my whistle'?

He drinks. Begins a speech:

When the Muses smile, no beams more warm the heart than those of dark Melpomene . . .

ALEX. Can I open my eyes?

TRIGG. No!

ALL. Ssh!

BLAGRAVE. . . . She of the tragic mode, whose song is the hush of the waiting crowd, whose breath is the pungent tang of paint and sawdust . . .

SHANK (*to* ROBINSON). I'll be ruined.

BLAGRAVE. . . . she whose wild domain, earthliest of Zeus' kingdoms but most heavenly, now I enter.

ROBINSON (*to* SHANK). You're right. You will.

SHANK. I know I bloody will.

SEVERAL. Ssh!

BLAGRAVE. Truth is always new and always startling. Truth in art is the crystal lens through which we behold the world new-born, as clear and bright as through the eye of a child. Tonight we saw, no squeaking puppet of impersonation, but a maiden. Treacherous, flawed, alluring, ripe with the lush outpouring of the feminine soul. We saw that half of God's good work as never before. To Stephen Hammerton.

Glasses are raised. STEPHEN *stands.*

STEPHEN. I never thought I wanted to act. And now I do. And it was all for Shanky.

Applause. He sits.

BLAGRAVE. To John Shank, the master pedagogue of the boards!

Glasses are raised: SHANK *half-stands.*

SEVERAL. John Shank.

SHANK. Most kind, most kind.

He sits. JHON, *who rose for the toast, remains standing:*

JHON. If I may add my ha'penny-worth? Now some of you younger lads won't know this . . .

SHANK (*mutters*). Christ.

JHON. . . . but Master Shank and I are the last two theatre men alive who carried the beams and timbers of old Master Burbage's theatre over the frozen Thames in 1600 . . .

SHANK. I was fourteen. I was a child, for God's sake!

JHON. There were bonfires. There were fireworks. There were skates and sleds. There were toboggans . . .

SHANK *joins in as he continues:*

. . . there was roasted codlings, there was . . .

JHON *fades out as* SHANK *continues in a curious rustic accent:*

SHANK. . . . traitors wiv their 'eads on pikes and Caffolicks 'anging upside down an' . . .

ROBINSON. Shut up.

BLAGRAVE. May I continue? Next, a player . . . at this table . . . known to us all . . .

SHANK (*quiet*). Spare the bastard.

BLAGRAVE. . . . Master Honey! A touch mature, perhaps as Sparta's queen? Adieu to the female line! Your manly voice and noble height will pave the path to many a sturdier role. To Master John Honyman!

He beams, looks around. Glasses are raised with some embarrassment.

SEVERAL. John Honyman.

HONEY *rises.*

HONEY. Thank you. Thank you most especially Master Blagrave. That was the nicest epitaph I could have wished for.

SHANK (*mutters to* ROBINSON). You'll be next.

ROBINSON (*mutters*). I don't believe this.

BLAGRAVE. Next, let us recall those heroines of a bygone age . . .

He turns to ROBINSON.

As Ben hath writ:

'There's Dickey Robinson, a very pretty fellow . . . '

ROBINSON. Thank you! Thank you!

BLAGRAVE.
    ' . . . Dressed like a lawyer's wife amongst them all,
    (I lent him clothes) but, to see him behave it . . . '

ROBINSON. Enough! Enough!

SHANK. Marvellous! Thank you!

> BLAGRAVE *continues, amid cries of 'Stop!', 'We've heard it!', etc.*

BLAGRAVE.
> ' . . . And lay the law: and carve; and drink unto them; then talk bawdy, and send frolics . . . !' (*etc.*)

> JHON *rises, sepulchral and impressive. He points a finger at* BLAGRAVE:

JHON. 'Ope not thy ponderous and marble jaws! But get thee to a nunnery! Go!'

BLAGRAVE (*highly amused*). I cede my place!

> *He sits. Good-natured cheers and applause.*

TRIGG (*to* ALEX). Open your eyes.

> ALEX *sees the heap of objects: he's appalled.*

ALEX. It's huge!

> *Cheers and applause.*

TRIGG. Give up?

TRIGG/JHON/HONEY/STEPHEN. Give up! Give up!

ALEX. I can do it! Count to five!

ROBINSON (*to* SHANK). We'll make it a hundred.

SHANK. What?

ROBINSON. The board will give you a hundred pounds for Stephen.

SHANK. You're mad.

> ROBINSON, *about to reply, gives up in the face of a chorus from the others, counting as* ALEX *furiously studies the heap of objects.*

TRIGG/JHON/HONEY/STEPHEN. One!

ROBINSON. Two hundred.

TRIGG/JHON/HONEY/STEPHEN. Two!

SHANK. You're raving.

TRIGG/HONEY/JHON/STEPHEN. Three!

ROBINSON. Three hundred.

TRIGG/HONEY/JHON/STEPHEN. Four!

SHANK. Can't hear you.

TRIGG/HONEY/JHON/STEPHEN. Five!

ROBINSON. We'll cancel the debt.

SHANK. What's that?

TRIGG/JHON/HONEY/STEPHEN (*to* ALEX). Time up!
Close your eyes! Go!

ALEX *starts his list, which continues till further notice.*

ALEX. Earwax-poker, wart-curette, one silver watch, penknife
horn handle, penknife broken, penknife, penknife, two
quills, paperknife, handkerchief moiré silk, one linen
mouchoir, length of twine, small tin of brickdust, two
pieces burnt cork, one piece red crayon, one tin henna,
Turkish toothbrush, bladder, pencil, notebook, prayer-book,
doorkey rusty, doorkey shiny, doorkey, doorkey, saltcellar,
pewter spoon, set of tables, three glass marbles: one dead
man's eye, one goon, one twirly wonder; shoehorn, one
bottle goosegrease, orange-peel teeth, two steam-bath
tokens, lover's bracelet, cloakpin, two steel pins, onion,
garlic, half an apple, medallion St. Genesius, medallion St.
Jude, rosary, ivory crucifix, three flints, three twists tobacco,
piece of kindling, snuffbox . . .

Meanwhile:

ROBINSON. We'll cancel the debt. We'll cancel the whole five
hundred pounds you owe the Company.

SHANK. For Stephen?

ROBINSON. Yes, for Stephen!

SHANK. After tonight?

ROBINSON. Especially after tonight. He's had an immense
success. Bigger than Honey. Bigger than me.

SHANK. Bollocks. I won't have it. Keep your money. It's an
outrage. It's a damned humiliation.

ROBINSON. Don't be a fool. You did your job. You've got a brilliant pupil.

SHANK. Not my pupil. I won't teach the little bastard. Never again. I'm selling him off to Master Blagrave.

STEPHEN. I won't go.

ALEX is struggling. TRIGG is holding a pair of spectacles before his closed eyes. But ALEX's brain has blown a fuse.

ALEX. One brass buckle.

TRIGG. And?

HONEY. Ssh!

He listens to SHANK and STEPHEN.

STEPHEN. I'm not going anywhere.

SHANK. You bloody well are.

TRIGG. One pair of . . . ?

HONEY. Ssh!

STEPHEN. You promised!

HONEY. What did he promise?

STEPHEN. He promised that I could stay if I was good. And I *was* good. Wasn't I?

HONEY (*to* SHANK). And I believed you.

STEPHEN. *Nobody* could have played that part like I did. *Nobody.*

To the table at large:

Isn't that so? Is there anyone? Anywhere else in London? They were *cheering! Cheering!*

SHANK rises in a fury.

SHANK. Go home!

STEPHEN. That isn't my home, you bastard!

SHANK. Out! Before I bend you over that chair and beat you!

STEPHEN. I'm not frightened! People have hit me hundreds of times. I've had nothing to eat and people pinching me and pulling my hair and saying I'm funny and peculiar and there's been nothing, ever, ever as bad as this!

SHANK. I'd sooner cut my throat than watch you act. I'd sooner watch a public execution. It was a total and utter betrayal of all I stand for.

STEPHEN. No it wasn't.

SHANK. I taught you something nobody gives a fuck about any longer Something nobody even knows existed. I taught you proper acting. Like it was done by people much greater than you or me. And you degraded it. You made it a thing to laugh at.

STEPHEN. No I didn't!

SHANK. Every fucking thing I said, you did the opposite.

STEPHEN. I did not. I did the verse the way you taught me. I did the gestures. And the feeling. And I wouldn't have changed a thing, except it suddenly seemed so stupid. If you're playing a woman, what's the point in being like anything else? I think it's *daft*.

SHANK *has heaved his bag on to the table. He pulls a document out and reads it out:*

SHANK. 'To wit: William Waverley, Master Brewer, hereby buys one Stephen Hammerton, boy.'

He passes the document to BLAGRAVE. *Reads another:*

'To wit: Master Waverley, Master Brewer, sells Stephen Hammerton, boy, to John Shank, actor, for thirty pounds.'

He passes the document to BLAGRAVE. *Pulls out a blank document. Recites, making it up:*

To wit: John Shank, actor, sells one Stephen Hammerton, boy, to Master William Blagrave, Deputy to the Master of the King's Revels, for the sum of . . .

He looks around the room:

. . . of . . . seventy pounds and half a crown.

BLAGRAVE (*of the documents in his hand*). Are these authentic? Are they truly signed?

SHANK. Does anyone say they're not?

Nobody does.

BLAGRAVE. Proceed.

He gives the documents back to SHANK.

SHANK. Pen. Ink.

BLAGRAVE *produces his briefcase with ink and pen, as in Scene One.* SHANK *jabs the pen in the ink and begins to write. Stops. Gets out his spectacles. Drops them. Stands in order to see the paper better. Carries on writing. Slows down. Puts his hand to his head. Stops.*

Something's happening.

He stands. Then falls, pole-axed, over the table. Chaos: all either scatter or rush to SHANK's *assistance. He's unconscious.* JHON *and* ROBINSON *carry him away and out of sight.* STEPHEN, TRIGG, ALEX, HONEY *and* BLAGRAVE *are left.*

Pause.

ALEX. I've got it.

HONEY. Ssh.

ALEX. Pair of spectacles.

STEPHEN. They're Jhon's.

TRIGG. So many Johns now.

STEPHEN. Honyman, Jhon and Shank.

To BLAGRAVE:

Could I please see that sheet of paper?

BLAGRAVE *looks at it.*

BLAGRAVE. It's unsigned.

He holds the paper to a candle. All watch as it burns. ROBINSON *comes back. To* HONEY:

ROBINSON. He's asking for you.

HONEY *nods, goes.* ROBINSON *turns to the boys:*

You boys will sleep at my house tonight. You all did well.

TRIGG. What happened?

ROBINSON. He's had an apoplexy.

TRIGG. Is it serious?

ROBINSON. It's serious for an actor. My wife will make up beds for you all. Tell her that I shall be home a little later.

TRIGG. What time?

ROBINSON. Just say, a little later. She'll understand.

TRIGG. Come on, Goffy.

BLAGRAVE. Good night, Trigg. Good night, Stephen.

STEPHEN. Good night, sir.

BLAGRAVE (*to* GOFFE). Good night.

ALEX *stares at him, bewildered.*

TRIGG. He's not too jolly either. Good night, sir.

They go. ROBINSON *and* BLAGRAVE *are left alone.*

ROBINSON. We should meet.

BLAGRAVE. Whenever you wish. Any advice you care to offer would be welcome.

ROBINSON. Thank you.

Pause.

ROBINSON. Personally, I always think it creates a bad impression when two competing theatres stage a similar play. We should compare our plans.

BLAGRAVE. Indeed.

Pause.

I serve two masters now. I often wonder why the phrase achieved such dark associations? It's a practical arrangement. Good night.

ROBINSON. Good night.

BLAGRAVE *goes.* ROBINSON *stays at the table.*

End of scene.

Scene Four

Winter.

*A fly-gallery runs left to right. We're in the flies of the
Blackfriars theatre.*

*STEPHEN is there. He wears the Queen of Spain costume
which HONEY was wearing when we first saw him. His wig
and make-up are more natural and becoming than HONEY's
were.*

*HONEY comes on slowly. He's costumed as a messenger. His
hair is short and he's grown a moustache. He looks shrunken
and ordinary.*

HONEY. Hello.

> STEPHEN *sees him.*

STEPHEN. Hello.

HONEY. What are you doing?

STEPHEN. Just waiting. Jhon doesn't think we'll get onstage
till after lunch.

> HONEY *joins him. Looks down towards the stage.*

Let me look at you.

HONEY. You see me every day.

STEPHEN. Not properly.

> HONEY *turns.* STEPHEN *looks at him.*

Your moustache is coming on well. Will you curl it up at
the ends?

HONEY. No.

STEPHEN. Why not?

HONEY. Because of the doubling.

STEPHEN. Oh. Oh yes, of course.

> *Pause.*

HONEY. I liked you at the run-through.

STEPHEN. Thank you.

HONEY. No, I did.

STEPHEN. Have you got any notes?

HONEY. No.

STEPHEN. I didn't want to copy your performance.

HONEY. Well you certainly don't do that.

STEPHEN. I'm looking forward to playing indoors. I've tried the throw. Dickie says the audience listens more carefully than they do at the Globe because they've paid more.

HONEY. He would say that.

STEPHEN. Oh, Dickie's all right.

HONEY. Is it true you're playing Juliet?

STEPHEN. Yes. In March.

HONEY. Do you know the other casting?

STEPHEN. No. Do you?

HONEY. No.

STEPHEN. I shouldn't worry. Most of the parts are good.

HONEY. I wasn't fishing.

STEPHEN. I didn't think you were.

HONEY. One finds one's level.

STEPHEN. Don't talk like that.

HONEY. It's true. I like it now. It's quieter, dressing with the men. I've more free time. The days fill up. I do the show, then a couple of drinks, then bed.

STEPHEN *looks at him.*

STEPHEN. Is it soft or bristly?

He puts out a finger to touch HONEY*'s moustache.*
HONEY *turns away.*

HONEY. Leave it.

STEPHEN. Sorry.

Pause.

I came up here to think about Shanky. I saw him again last night. It was wild. He kept on shouting.

HONEY. At you?

STEPHEN. No, not at me. Out of the window, mostly. Then just as I was about to go, he said, 'Good bye, old son. You had your chance at last.' I thought, oh well, at least he's lucid. Then he asked me to forgive him.

HONEY. For trying to sell you?

STEPHEN. I couldn't exactly work it out. And so I mumbled something reassuring. He was quieter after that. I think he thought I was someone else.

He looks down.

They're going to rehearse the change. I love this bit.

They watch.

HONEY. There's Trigg. He's got in the way again. (*Quietly.*) Get off, you idiot.

STEPHEN. He's never going to get that saucepan laugh.

HONEY. Alex moves.

STEPHEN. Not any more.

HONEY. Then it's the line. It isn't funny.

STEPHEN. Oh, I don't know. 'Saucepan''s funny. If you say it right. Look, they're starting.

Music is heard from below, as for a splendid entracte. Sounds of a smooth scene-change from below, and a changing light.

STEPHEN. The forest dissolves. The clouds fly out. The Spanish galleon sails into view on a shining ocean.

Clouds fly up from below. SHANK reclines on one of them, as in the first scene, but feebler. He looks down towards the stage.

SHANK. A ship. A bright blue sea dotted with tiny islands. What will they think of next? No sign of imps. Until I feel the malevolent prod of tridents . . . here I'll stay. Won't budge. They'll have to drag me down. Last week I dream of Saloman Pavy. His mattress next to mine. I kept him chatting all night. Easy enough to do. He'd never an atom of concentration. On and on we talked. My friend. My pal. All down the room, the other boys were shushing us. I didn't care. I had my plan. Then as the dawn came up, his face went white. He said. 'Oh Johnny, I'm so frightened, I should have been learning my lines.' 'Don't worry', I said, 'you know them.' Knowing he didn't. Knowing I did. Last night he came to see me. Looking the same as he always did, not even older. 'You got your chance at last,' I said. 'What was I like?', he asked me. 'Good', I said. 'Quite marvellous. In your own peculiar way.' And then I asked him to forgive me. And he did. He said he loved me. And he cried. We both did.

The music changes: it's rapt, magical. The cloud starts to move up.

We're moving. Up? That can't be bad. What will it be this time?

The cloud moves higher.

I'll dream of angels.

The cloud ascends out of sight, and SHANK *with it. A spatter of applause from actors and stagehands below.*

Pause.

HONEY. Let's go.

STEPHEN. Let's stay. They'll call us.

They wait.

End of play.

Afterword

All but one of the characters in *Cressida* existed. Details of
their lives are recorded in wills, in letters, in chance remarks
by 17th-century theatre-goers and (most of all) in reports of
the incredibly complex lawsuits which soaked up so much of
their time and money.

At the time that the play is set, their theatre company, the
King's Men, was the richest and most prestigious in London.
Its patron was Charles I, who often invited the company to
play at Court. Its senior actors helped rehearse his Royal
Masques and when plague broke out, closing the public
theatres and wiping out the takings, the company received
a handout from the King to tide it over.

But its favoured status was about to end. From now on, the
country would be rocked by a series of constitutional crises,
each one leaving the Royal patron weaker than before. After
the King's Men's final appearance at Court, on January 6th,
1642, the Master of the King's Revels, Sir Henry Herbert,
wrote in his daybook:

'On Twelfe Night . . . the prince had a play called 'The Scornful
Lady' at the Cockpitt, but the kinge and queene were not there;
and it was the only play acted at court in the whole Christmas.'

Two days before the show, Charles had led a posse of cavalry
to Westminster in an attempt to arrest his five main enemies in
the House of Commons. But they'd gone missing. 'I see all the
birds are flown,' he said, before retreating in disgrace. He'd
lost control of London: it's no wonder he couldn't face the
play. The performance must have been a tense one and it's easy
to imagine the gloom in the dressing-room. 'Dreadful house!'
'Not a laugh!'. The following week, the King left London, not
to return until his trial and execution seven years later.

After the *Scornful Lady* debacle, the King's Men staggered on
for a few more months. But they were now wholly reliant on
their box-office takings, and these were plummeting: crises are

bad for business. And in September, Parliament closed the
theatres.

The King's Men dispersed, never to reassemble. Thomas
Pollard and another actor stole the costumes, hangings and
playbooks and 'converted them to their own use.' When Civil
War broke out, several of the actors took up arms; all except
for Eilart Swanston backed the King.

John Shank was a long-standing member of the King's Men,
though the date he joined them isn't known. He was best-
known for his 'jig', presumably a comic dance which he
performed at the end of the show. As in the play, he made a
speciality of buying, training and renting-out boy-players: they
included Thomas Pollard, John Thompson and John Honyman.

The circumstances of his death were more complicated than
I've shown. Most of the original actors from the golden age of
Shakespeare and Richard Burbage had left their shares in the
company to their immediate families, none of whom made any
artistic contribution: they simply raked in their share of the
profits. Two senior actors, John Taylor and Joseph Lowin, were
eventually allowed to buy shares, but the rest of the company
had to get by on a wage, albeit a very good one. This led to
great dissatisfaction and, in 1635, three of the younger actors,
Swanston, Pollard and Robert Benfield, petitioned Sir Henry
Herbert to be included in the share-out.

What they didn't know was that Shank, far from showing solid-
arity with his fellow-players, had meanwhile secretly approached
the son of the distinguished actor Thomas Heminges, and bought
the shares which Heminges Junior had inherited at his father's
death. When this got out, the other actors were furious and Shank
was 'restrained from the stage'. His will is a masterpiece of
acrimony, full of complaints about the vast expense to which
his boys have put him and warnings about the double-dealings
of his colleagues. He was buried at St. Giles, Cripplegate on
27 January 1636. His widow married a man called Fitche.

Richard Robinson remained an actor up to the closure of the
theatres, but seems to have played only supporting roles. He
was rich, thanks to his marriage to a major shareholder, and
built up a noted art-collection. He died in 1648.

A man named Blagrave was a part-time Warder at the Tower of London, so it's possible that the arts-bureaucrat-cum-commercial-impresario was holding down yet a third job. He certainly wasn't bothered by the obvious conflict of interest between the two jobs we know about. In 1634, the King's Men planned a new play, *The Lancashire Witches*, timed to coincide with the sensational London trial of the witches of Pendle. Blagrave promptly announced the revival of an old play, *Dr. Dee*, hastily re-titled *Dr. Dee and the Witches*: a blatant spoiler, as the King's Men pointed out when they petitioned Sir Henry Herbert to stop the production. Sir Henry referred the case to none other than Blagrave himself, whose verdict is unknown. He continued his double role until 1635, after which no more is heard of him.

Jhon is invented, though a stage-hand of that name, thus spelt, is mentioned in one of the surviving 'plots', i.e. running orders of exits and entrances, pinned up backstage as an aide memoire to the cast.

Little is know about the boys. They must have acquitted themselves well onstage, or why would the playwrights have written them such huge and demanding roles? But they aren't much documented, and one gets the curious impression that almost nobody in the business really noticed them or thought of them as human beings, as opposed to valuable but short-lived commodities. The exception to this indifference is Ben Jonson, who wrote a beautiful poem on the death of Salamon Pavy, taught the classics to Nathan Field (another child-victim of the great kidnapping scandal of 1599), paid Robinson the compliment of putting him in *The Devil is an Ass* and scattered small but charming references to boy actors throughout his other plays.

What we know of Stephen Hammerton comes mostly from a law-suit between the King's Men and William Blagrave, both of whom claimed to have bought him. The King's Men's title to him relied, as in *Cressida*, on a transparent boy-laundering scam involving one Master Waverley of the Strand. Sir Henry seems to have bent the rules in this case, as Hammerton remained with the King's Men and his career went from strength to strength. 'A most noted and beautiful Woman actor,' said a contemporary, 'who afterwards acted, with equal grace and applause, a Young Lover's Part.'

John Honyman died three months after John Shank. He left ten shillings to each of his fellow-actors to buy rings in his memory, twenty shillings to be distributed among the poor of Cripplegate and the rest to his mother.

William Trigg stayed with the King's Men as long as they lasted. At the outbreak of the Civil War he joined the Royal forces, rising to the rank of Captain. Towards the end of the war he changed sides, as a result of which he had various abusive squibs written about him.

Alexander Goffe became a publisher.

Richard Gunnell died pursued by creditors in 1634.

When the theatres re-opened at the time of the Restoration, after a lay-off of 18 years, only a handful of old stagers were alive or well enough to return to the boards. The strange convention – unique in Europe – of boys cross-dressing to play women had vanished for ever. The only real survivor was Sir Henry Herbert, who took up his old post as Master of the Revels as insouciantly as if he had never been interrupted. Under the Theatres Act of 1737, the powers of his office were transferred to the Lord Chamberlain, who continued to exercise them until 1968.

Nicholas Wright